MORE AUTHORS AND ILLUSTRATORS THROUGH THE YEAR

Ready-to-Use Literature Activities for Grades K-3

David J. Fiday

THE CENTER FOR APPLIED RESEARCH IN EDUCATION
West Nyack, New York 10995

© 1992 by

THE CENTER FOR APPLIED
RESEARCH IN EDUCATION

West Nyack, New York 10995

All rights reserved. Permission is given for individual classroom teachers and library media specialists to reproduce the activity sheets and illustrations for classroom use. Reproduction of these materials for an entire school system is strictly forbidden.

10 9 8 7 5 4 4 3 2

GRAPHICS BY "THE PRINT SHOP" BRODERBUND SOFTWARE INC., 1984.
Crossword puzzles created with "Crossword Magic" by Mindscape, 1981.
Word search puzzles created with "Puzzles and Posters" by MECC, 1983.

```
Library of Congress Cataloging-in-Publication Data

Fiday, David.
    More authors and illustrators through the year : ready-to-use
  literature activities for grades K-3 / David J. Fiday.
       p.   cm.
    Continues: Authors and illustrators through the year.
    Includes bibliographical references and index.
    ISBN 0-87628-576-0
    1. School libraries--Activity programs.  2. Libraries, Children's-
  -Activity programs.  3. Children's literature--Study and teaching
  (Primary)  4. Children's literature--Illustrations.  5. Children-
  -Books and reading.   I. Fiday, David. Authors and illustrators
  through the year.   II. Title.
  Z675.S3F453  1992
  027.8'222--dc20                                            91-46032
                                                                  CIP
```

C5760-8
ISBN 0-87628-576-0

**The Center for Applied
Research in Education**
Business Information & Publishing Division
West Nyack, NY 10995

Simon & Schuster, A Paramount Communications Company

Printed in the United States of America

This book is dedicated to:

Joseph John and Vera Lou Fiday,
my parents and first teachers.
Love eternal for your love and
support through all these years.

Further dedicated to:

authors, illustrators, editors,
parents, and teachers who give
great stories to children.

But most of all to:

Jennifer and Jessica
all my love,

Dad

ABOUT THE AUTHOR

David Fiday earned his B.A. and M.A. degrees in Instructional Technology from Northern Illinois University in DeKalb. He has done graduate work with computers and has taught computer seminars and classes for a local junior college and university. David has been a media specialist since 1975, working in the Bolingbrook and Laraway school districts in Illinois. He is currently the media director for the Palos East Elementary School in Palos Heights, Illinois.

David has published articles and stories in various teacher, computer, and children's magazines. He co-authored *Time to Go* with Beverly Fiday (Harcourt Brace Jovanovich, 1990), and wrote *Sweet Surprises* (Standard Publishing, 1989), and *Authors and Illustrators Through the Year* (The Center for Applied Research in Education, 1989).

About This Resource

More Authors and Illustrators Through the Year continues the promise and purpose of *Authors and Illustrators Through the Year.* It brings children and good books together under the helpful direction of K-3 classroom teachers and library media specialists. It offers classroom teachers and library media specialists the opportunity to let children read good books at or near their reading level and develop a most important life-long attitude—reading for pleasure.

Students can easily read, write, and draw their way through the year using the more than 130 book titles and accompanying ready-to-use, reproducible activity sheets included in this book. More than 100 new authors and illustrators are introduced in this volume. There is also an added emphasis on writing activities, as well as the inclusion of multicultural titles which deal with other cultures and ethnic groups.

Contents

Each month includes:
- A monthly table of contents listing the authors and/or illustrators, their books, and activities to extend students' reading/listening experiences. All multicultural titles are indicated by asterisks in each month's contents.
- An author sheet listing the authors of that month with their birthdates, whether they are an author and/or illustrator, and a suggested reading/listening level.
- Activity sheets that can be reproduced as many times as needed, including reading activities (fill-in-the-blanks, word searches, crossword puzzles, story sequence), writing activities (group story projects, individual stories, short-answer, poem-writing, personal information), and drawing activities.
- Gold Star bookmarks to encourage reading and to promote that month's authors.
- A complete answer key to that month's activity sheets.
- Bibliographies of that month's authors.

The last portion of the book includes the following helpful appendices:

- An alphabetical listing of authors/illustrators
- A chronological listing of authors/illustrators by their birthdates
- An alphabetical listing of titles
- A listing of all titles by topics

How to Use

After you have created the calendar, introduce your children to its use. Here are a few ways to start:

1. Children may view the calendar and select an author's book to find. They read the book and complete the worksheet.
2. Specific titles might be read to the children.
3. Library media specialists may suggest specific titles and activity sheets for classroom use by teachers.
4. When a short period of time exists in the daily schedule, a great story and a follow-up activity are the perfect solutions.
5. Children may select an author of a series and read all of his or her books.
6. If some children share a birthday with an author or illustrator, they may want to read books by "their author or illustrator" first.
7. Each child reads his or her birthday author (or one near his or her birthday), gives a book report, and has a classmate read the book. This sharing and swapping encourages and motivates reading.

For the Classroom Teacher

Teachers in self-contained elementary classrooms may want to create a reading support program with the materials contained in this book. Here are additional ways to incorporate trade books into your present reading program:

1. Tell the children you are going to give them their own "Authors' Reading Corner." Create the calendar, make a display, and designate an area (reading table, corner, or carpeted area) in which the children will read their books and do their activities.
2. Display selected titles from the month and place copies of the activity sheets in nearby folders. Label each folder with the title of the book.
3. Read one book to the children and complete the activity sheet with them.
4. Explain to the children that they may read any title and complete the activity sheet when you are working with another reading group.
5. Explain any other optional times (before lunch, after recess, when other assignments are complete, etc.) they may use the "Authors' Reading Corner."
6. Change the collection each month.

For the Library Media Specialist

More Authors and Illustrators Through the Year is a large resource. As such, the manner of organization can be a large-scale or simple operation depending on your particular needs. Copies of the activity sheets can be kept in file folders. When a child selects a specific author, the activity sheet can be given to the student at the same time. More able children may select their own worksheet after they have read a book.

A Final Word

This edition of *More Authors and Illustrators Through the Year* is a compendium, a gift from many people who love children and storytelling. I hope this new collection will extend the love of reading that started in volume one. Read on, forever!

David J. Fiday

How to Use the Gold Star Bookmark Program

The Gold Star Reading Incentive Program (monthly bookmarks) is designed to promote the reading of many authors each month. As children develop the reading habit, it is often a challenge to find new authors or titles to instantly satisfy their reading appetites. Having a ready-to-use bookmark program on hand is a boon to today's busy library media specialists and classroom teachers.

Children are rewarded for their reading when a gold foil star is placed over the open star on each bookmark after they have read a book by that author. For younger students, a star is awarded when a teacher, parent, or sibling reads a specific author's book to them.

For kindergarten or first graders, a large wall-sized bookmark allows children to see their progress toward reading the selected authors each month. It is also a helpful lesson plan reminder for teachers and library media specialists who love reading good books to children every day.

How to Use

Photocopy the appropriate bookmark page for the month. Explain its use to the children. Before doing so, decide on these ideas:

- Will you give a gold star for each author read?
- Or will you color it in with a gold marker?
- Or have children color it with a yellow crayon by themselves?

For example, read a book by a September author, such as *Danny and the Dinosaur* by Syd Hoff. Give each child a gold star. Tell the children that they will (name one of the three options) each time they read a book or have it read to them. This is an exciting way to introduce the program.

Children should:

1. Cut out Primary Set 1 and Primary Set 2 bookmarks.
2. Glue the back sides together.
3. Find and read titles by those authors.
4. Take the bookmark to the teacher for the star or to color in the star.

The Intermediate bookmarks are designed for children reading at or above the third-grade level. With the emphasis on reading skills, it is only a matter of time before a majority of our second and third graders are reading above their grade level as a group. Third-grade teachers may want to share the Intermediate bookmarks with fourth- and fifth-grade teachers for use with their reluctant readers.

When the same author appears on a Primary and Intermediate bookmark, he or she crosses grade levels. For example, Judith Viorst writes for all children aged 4–10 and higher. Other examples are Judy Blume, Judy Delton, and Patricia Reilly Giff. Poets, such as Jack Prelutsky and Lee Bennett Hopkins also cross grade levels.

For the Classroom Teacher

The Gold Star Reading Incentive Program can be used in conjunction with your Author of the Month display, if you choose.

Some children love to read every available book by their favorite authors. Blank bookmarks are provided for you and your students to create your own author-specific bookmarks. Here is an example:

Else Holmelund Minarik
☆ A kiss for Little Bear
☆ Little Bear
☆ Little Bear's Friend
☆ Little Bear's Visit

How to Use the Gold Star Bookmark Program

For the Library Media Specialist

Create a Bookmark of the Month display in the library media center. Tell the children they may use books from the public library, home or other sources that were written by any author on the bookmark.

Encourage the children to create their own bookmarks. They can:

1. Write the names of books available as listed in the card catalog. They can write them in alphabetical order, which reinforces alphabetizing skills.
2. Place a star in front of the title.
3. Read a title and color in the star.
4. Select a new author and duplicate the process starting in step 1.

BLANK BOOKMARKS

How to Make the Calendar

Calendar Idea One

1. Use two oversized calendars available from a teacher supply store or make them from posterboard. Hang two calendars each month to offer children a variety of authors. Start the school year with August and September, and include July at the end of the school year in June.
2. Cut blank catalog cards or unlined 3" × 5" index cards to 2" × 2" squares that fit within each daily space.
3. Use a hole punch to make a hole in the card in the appropriate spot as shown in the illustration.

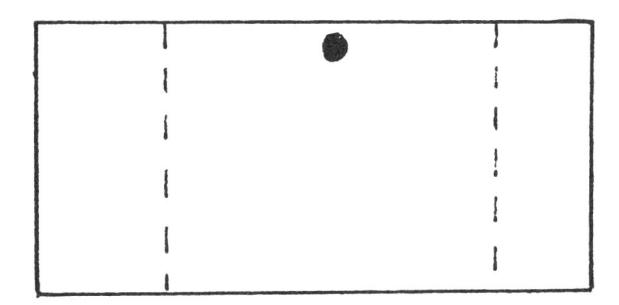

4. Write the date and the author's name as shown in the illustration.

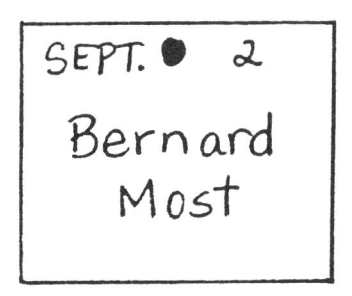

> SEPT. ● 2
> Bernard
> Most

5. Stick pins into the date squares and hang the appropriate authors' birthdates in sequence. This moveable card format allows you to easily change the authors each month.

6. You might want to add a "Happy Birthday" banner (either store-bought or teacher-made) to increase the atmosphere of celebration. A "Happy Birthday Authors and Illustrators" banner can also be made with certain computer software programs such as "Print Shop," available from Broderbund Software, 17 Paul Drive, San Rafael, CA 94903.

Calendar Idea Two

You might want to focus on a "(month's) Featured Authors" display. The computer program called "Print Shop Companion" can be used to make a calendar similar to the one shown here.

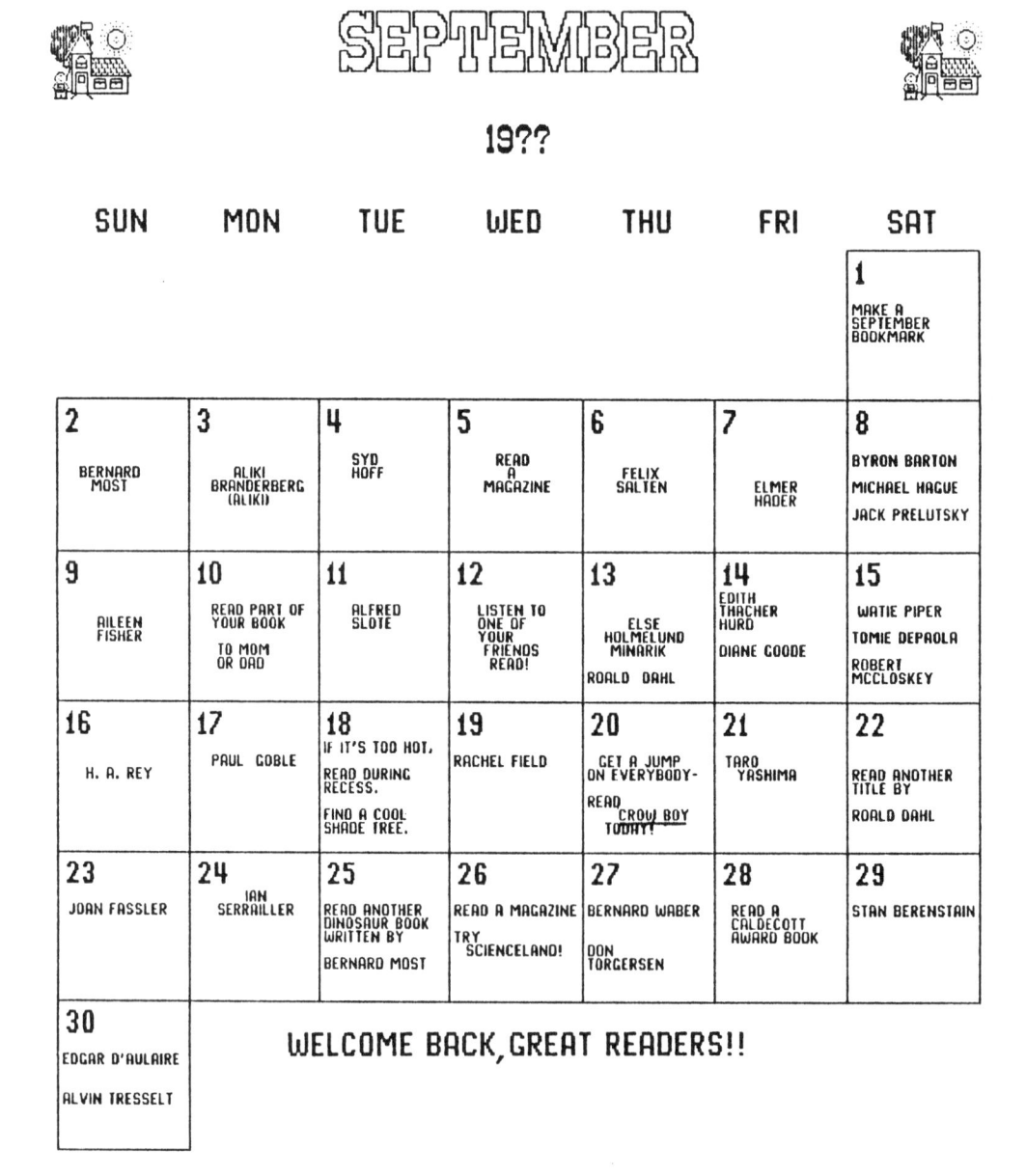

SEPTEMBER 19??

SUN	MON	TUE	WED	THU	FRI	SAT
						1 MAKE A SEPTEMBER BOOKMARK
2 BERNARD MOST	**3** ALIKI BRANDERBERG (ALIKI)	**4** SYD HOFF	**5** READ A MAGAZINE	**6** FELIX SALTEN	**7** ELMER HADER	**8** BYRON BARTON / MICHAEL HAGUE / JACK PRELUTSKY
9 AILEEN FISHER	**10** READ PART OF YOUR BOOK TO MOM OR DAD	**11** ALFRED SLOTE	**12** LISTEN TO ONE OF YOUR FRIENDS READ!	**13** ELSE HOLMELUND MINARIK / ROALD DAHL	**14** EDITH THACHER HURD / DIANE GOODE	**15** WATIE PIPER / TOMIE DEPAOLA / ROBERT MCCLOSKEY
16 H. A. REY	**17** PAUL GOBLE	**18** IF IT'S TOO HOT, READ DURING RECESS. FIND A COOL SHADE TREE.	**19** RACHEL FIELD	**20** GET A JUMP ON EVERYBODY- READ CROW BOY TODAY!	**21** TARO YASHIMA	**22** READ ANOTHER TITLE BY ROALD DAHL
23 JOAN FASSLER	**24** IAN SERRAILLER	**25** READ ANOTHER DINOSAUR BOOK WRITTEN BY BERNARD MOST	**26** READ A MAGAZINE TRY SCIENCELAND!	**27** BERNARD WABER / DON TORGERSEN	**28** READ A CALDECOTT AWARD BOOK	**29** STAN BERENSTAIN
30 EDGAR D'AULAIRE / ALVIN TRESSELT						

WELCOME BACK, GREAT READERS!!

How to Make the Calendar

   Copies of this calendar can be given to children for individual use. Print the filled-in calendar on one side of the paper, and a blank calendar on the other side. The students can then color in with crayon the squares of the authors they read. If they choose, students can use the blank calendar as follows:

- Write the last name of the author read in today's date.
- Color the square.
- If more than one author is read in a day, write all their last names in the date square and color it.
- Books from home, those from friends, or those given as gifts could also be included on the calendar.

Contents

About This Resource v
How to Use the Gold Star Bookmark Program ix
How to Make the Calendar xiii

SEPTEMBER • 1

September Authors Sheet 2
Activity Sheets (* denotes multicultural titles)

    Demi, *Liang and the Magic Paintbrush**
    Aliki Brandenberg, *Digging Up Dinosaurs*
    Byron Barton, *Buzz, Buzz, Buzz*
    John Scieszka, *The True Story of the 3 Little Pigs*
    Michael Hague, *Alphabears*
    Anthony Browne, *Willy the Wimp*
    Diane Goode, *I Hear a Noise*
    John Steptoe, *Mufaro's Beautiful Daughters**
    Tomie DePaola, *The Legend of the Indian Paintbrush**
    Donald Hall, *The Ox-Cart Man*
    Hans Wilhelm, *I'll Always Love You*
    Taro Yashima, *The Umbrella**

September Bookmarks 15
September Answer Key 16
September Authors Bibliography 17

OCTOBER • 19

October Authors Sheet 20
Activity Sheets (* denotes multicultural titles)

    Reeve Lindbergh, *Midnight Farm*
    John Himmelman, *Amanda and the Witch Switch*
    Edward Ormondroyd, *Broderick*
    Karen Ackerman, *Song and Dance Man*
    Robert D. San Souci, *The Legend of Scarface**
    Robert D. San Souci, *The Talking Eggs**

    Polly Cameron, *I Can't Said the Ant*
    Lulu Delacre, *Arroz Con Leche**
    Janet Ahlberg, *The Jolly Postman or Other People's Letters*
    Paula Winter, *The Bear & the Fly*
    Cyndy Szekeres, *Moving Day*

October Bookmarks 32
October Answer Key 33
October Authors Bibliography 34

NOVEMBER • 35

November Authors Sheet 36
Activity Sheets (* denotes multicultural titles)

    Gail Haley, *A Story, a Story**
    Lois Ehlert, *Eating the Alphabet: Fruits and Vegetables from A to Z*
    Nathaniel Benchley, *The Strange Disappearance of Arthur Cluck*
    Alan Baker, *Benjamin's Portrait*
    Jean Fritz, *Who's That Stepping on Plymouth Rock?*
    Margaret Musgrove, *Ashanti to Zulu**
    Ann H. Scott, *Sam**
    William Cole, *Poem Stew*
    Kevin Henkes, *Once Around the Block*
    Ed Young, *Lon Po Po**
    Stephanie Calmenson, *The Principal's New Clothes*

November Bookmarks 48
November Answer Key 49
November Authors Bibliography 50

DECEMBER • 53

December Authors Sheet 54
Activity Sheets (* denotes multicultural titles)

    Jan Brett, *Beauty and the Beast*
    David Macaulay, *Black and White*
    Hugh Lewin, *Jafta's Father**
    Phyllis Adams, *Hi, Dog!*
    Ellen Weiss, *Millicent Maybe*
    Adelaide Holl, *Rain Puddle*
    Barbara Gregorich, *Nine Men Chase a Hen*
    Ruth Stiles Gannett, *My Father's Dragon*
    Jerry Pinkney, *Pretend You're a Cat**
    Ted Rand, *Country Crossing*
    Molly Bang, *Ten, Nine, Eight**

Contents   xix

December Bookmarks **67**
December Answer Key.. **68**
December Authors Bibliography....................................... **69**

JANUARY • 71

January Authors Sheet **72**
Activity Sheets (* denotes multicultural titles)

    Barbara Williams, *Kevin's Grandma*
    Fernando Krahn, *Mystery of the Giant Footprints*
    Kay Chorao, *George Told Kate*
    Clyde Robert Bulla, *Dandelion Hill*
    Ann Tompert, *Grandfather Tang's Story**
    Margaret Hillert, *Dear Dragon*
    Brian Wildsmith, *The Lazy Bear*
    Ann Jonas, *Reflections; Round Trip; The Trek*
    Vera B. Williams, *"More, More, More," Said the Baby**
    Tony Johnston, *Happy Birthday, Mole and Troll*

January Bookmarks... **83**
January Answer Key **84**
January Authors Bibliography **86**

FEBRUARY • 89

February Authors Sheet **90**
Activity Sheets (* denotes multicultural titles)

    Rebecca Caudill, *A Certain Small Shepherd*
    Judith Viorst, *Alexander & the Terrible, Horrible, No Good, Very Bad Day*
    Judith Viorst, *The Tenth Good Thing About Barney*
    Franz Brandenberg, *"The Scare" from Leo and Emily's Big Ideas*
    Stephen Gammell, *The Relatives Came*
    David Small, *Imogene's Antlers*
    Mary Blount Christian, *The Pet Day Mystery**
    True Kelley/Kelly Oechsli, *Mice at Bat*
    Henry Wadsworth Longfellow, *Hiawatha**
    Henry Wadsworth Longfellow, *"Jemima"*
    Uri Shulevitz, *The Magician**
    David R. Collins, *Grandfather Woo Goes to School**

February Bookmarks.. **103**
February Answer Key **104**
February Authors Bibliography **106**

MARCH • 109

March Authors Sheet 110
Activity Sheets (* denotes multicultural titles)

    Barbara Berger, *Grandfather Twilight; When the Sun Rose*
    Barbara Berger, *Gwinna*
    Lonzo Anderson, *Two Hundred Rabbits*
    Mem Fox, *Guess What?*
    Thacher Hurd, *Mama Don't Allow*
    Kathleen Hague, *Bear Hugs*
    Wanda Gag, *Millions of Cats*
    Ezra Jack Keats, *Goggles**
    Ellen Raskin, *Nothing Ever Happens on My Block*
    Lilian Moore, *See My Lovely Poison Ivy*
    Douglas Florian, *Turtle Day*
    Byrd Baylor, *I'm in Charge of Celebrations**
    Charles Keller, *Tongue Twisters*

March Bookmarks... 124
March Answer Key 125
March Authors Bibliography 126

APRIL • 129

April Authors Sheet 130
Activity Sheets (* denotes multicultural titles)

    Jan Wahl, *Humphrey's Bear*
    Peter Collington, *The Angel and the Soldier Boy; On Christmas Eve*
    Tony Palazzo, *Timothy Turtle*
    Ruth Chew, *No Such Thing as a Witch*
    Nigel Gray, *A Country Far Away**
    Trina Schart Hyman, *Little Red Riding Hood*
    Clare Turlay Newberry, *April's Kittens*
    Kurt Wiese, *Fish in the Air**
    Eileen Christelow, *Five Little Monkeys Jumping on the Bed*
    Alvin Schwartz, *In a Dark, Dark Room and Other Scary Stories*
    Edith Baer, *This Is the Way We Go to School**
    Nicole Rubel, *Uncle Henry and Aunt Henrietta's Honeymoon*
    Maria Leach, *The Thing at the Foot of the Bed*

April Bookmarks.. 145
April Answer Key 146
April Authors Bibliography 147

Contents xxi

MAY • 149

May Authors Sheet 150
Activity Sheets (* denotes multicultural titles)

    Mavis Jukes, *Like Jake and Me*
    Giulio Maestro, *Ferryboat*
    Bruce Coville, *Sarah's Unicorn; Sarah and the Dragon*
    Eloise Greenfield, *Honey, I Love**
    Phyllis Halloran, *Cat Purrs*
    Peter Parnall, *The Great Fish**
    Brock Cole, *The Giant's Toe*
    Millicent Selsam, *Terry and the Caterpillars*
    Elaine Moore, *Mixed-Up Sam*
    Elizabeth Coatsworth, *The Cat Who Went to Heaven**

May Bookmarks 161
May Answer Key 162
May Authors Bibliography 164

JUNE • 167

June Authors Sheet 168
Activity Sheets (* denotes multicultural titles)

    Allan Ahlberg, *Funnybones*
    Cynthia Rylant, *Night in the Country*
    Gwendolyn Brooks, *Bronzeville Boys and Girls**
    Judith Elkin, *A Family in Japan**
    Maurice Sendak, *Chicken Soup with Rice*
    Robert Munsch, *Love You Forever*
    Bobbie Hamsa, *Your Pet Elephant*
    Bruce Degen, *The Magic Schoolbus Inside the Human Body*
    Dorothy Haas, *Peanut Butter and Jelly Series: New Friends*
    Pat Hutchins, *The Wind Blew*
    Jean Marzollo, *39 Kids on the Block: The Best Present Ever*
    Lynd Ward, *The Biggest Bear*
    Lucille Clifton, *The Boy Who Didn't Believe in Spring**

June Bookmarks 185
June Answer Key 186
June Authors Bibliography 187

JULY • 189

July Authors Sheet 190
Activity Sheets (* denotes multicultural titles)

> Stephen Mooser, *My Halloween Boyfriend*
> Fred Gwynne, *A Chocolate Moose for Dinner*
> James Stevenson, *Emma*
> Marcia Brown, *Shadow**
> Laura Joffe Numeroff, *If You Give a Mouse a Cookie*
> Arnold Adoff, *In for Winter, Out for Spring**
> Ida DeLage, *The Farmer and the Witch*
> Amy Ehrlich, *Bunnies All Day Long*
> Charlotte Pomerantz, *The Chalk Doll**
> Ron Barrett, *Animals Should Definitely Not Act Like People*
> Stephen Cosgrove, *Shimmeree*
> Natalie Babbitt, *The Devil's Storybook*

July Bookmarks.. 204
July Answer Key 205
July Authors Bibliography 206

AUGUST • 209

August Authors Sheet 210
Activity Sheets (* denotes multicultural titles)

> Mary Calhoun, *Jack and the Whoopie Wind*
> Nancy White Carlstrom, *Better Not Get Wet, Jesse Bear*
> Barbara Cooney, *Island Boy*
> Patricia McKissack, *Mirandy and Brother Wind**
> Jose Aruego/Adriane Dewey Aruego, *How the Sun Was Brought Back to the Sky*
> Don Freeman, *Corduroy; A Pocket for Corduroy**
> Joanna Cole, *Bony Legs**
> Audrey Wood, *Heckedy Peg*
> X.J. Kennedy, *Brats*
> Bernard Wiseman, *Morris Tells Boris Mother Moose Stories and Rhymes*
> Graham Oakley, *The Church Mice at Bay*
> Beau Gardner, *The Look Again . . . and Again, and Again, and Again Book*

August Bookmarks 223
August Answer Key 224
August Authors Bibliography 226

APPENDICES • 229

Alphabetical Authors 231
Authors by Birthdates 233
Title Index 235
Topical Index 239

SEPTEMBER

September 2   Demi, *Liang and the Magic Paintbrush* (writing activity)*

September 3   Aliki Brandenberg, *Digging Up Dinosaurs* (fossil sequence)

September 8   Byron Barton, *Buzz, Buzz, Buzz* (wordsearch)

September 8   John Scieszka, *The True Story of the 3 Little Pigs* (writing activity)

September 8   Michael Hague, *Alphabears* (writing activity)

September 11   Anthony Browne, *Willy the Wimp* (muscle research)

September 14   Diane Goode, *I Hear a Noise* (writing activity)

September 14   John Steptoe, *Mufaro's Beautiful Daughters* (writing activity)*

September 15   Tomie de Paola, *The Legend of the Indian Paintbrush* (drawing activity)*

September 20   Donald Hall, *Ox-Cart Man* (history research)

September 21   Hans Wilhelm, *I'll Always Love You* (writing activity)

September 21   Taro Yashima, *The Umbrella* (writing activity)*

September Bookmarks
September Answer Key
September Authors Bibliography

*Denotes multicultural title/activity

SEPTEMBER AUTHORS

DATE	NAME	AUTHOR/ILLUSTRATOR		K	1	2	3
				READING LEVEL			
2	Demi	X	X	X	X	X	
2	Bernard Most	X	X	X	X	X	
3	Aliki Brandenberg	X	X		X	X	X
4	Syd Hoff	X	X	X	X	X	
8	Byron Barton	X	X			X	X
8	Michael Hague		X				
8	Jack Prelutsky	X		X	X	X	X
11	Anthony Browne	X	X	X	X	X	
13	Roald Dahl	X					X
14	John Steptoe	X				X	X
14	Diane Goode	X	X	X	X	X	
15	Tomie de Paola	X	X	X	X	X	
15	Robert McCloskey	X	X		X	X	X
16	Janet Schulman	X					X
16	H.A. Rey	X	X	X	X	X	
17	Paul Goble	X	X			X	X
20	Donald Hall	X				X	X
21	Hans Wilhelm	X		X	X	X	
21	Taro Yashima	X	X	X	X	X	X
27	Bernard Waber	X	X	X	X	X	
27	Donald Torgersen	X				X	X
29	Stan Berenstain	X	X	X	X	X	
30	Edgar d'Aulaire	X	X			X	X

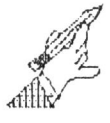

DEMI

Liang and the Magic Paintbrush

Read *Liang and the Magic Paintbrush*. Liang's paintings came to life. He drew presents for his friends. What gifts would you draw for your friends? Fill in the first blank with the gift and the second blank with the name of a friend. Write about each gift on the lines below. Draw your pictures for your friends on other pieces of paper. Use crayons, color pencils, pastels, or water colors like Demi!

If you liked this Chinese story, try *Chinese Mother Goose Rhymes* selected by Robert Wyndham (Putnam, 1989).

A _____ for _____

_____

_____

_____

_____

_____

_____

_____

Name _____ Date _____

ALIKI BRANDENBERG
Digging Up Dinosaurs

Read *Digging Up Dinosaurs*. Aliki tells us how fossils are created and unearthed. Name the steps and draw your own picture to go with each.

1. _____

   _____

2. _____

   _____

3. _____

   _____

4. _____

   _____

5. _____

   _____

6. _____

   _____

Name _____ **Date** _____

BYRON BARTON
Buzz Buzz Buzz

Read *Buzz Buzz Buzz*. Find and circle the words from the Word Bank in the flower below. Watch out for the bee!

```
F A R M E R G
A T U S D O G
S L O R A W E
E O I M I B E
G B E E M T I
O U Y U C O W
A L O B N A H
T L W I F E T
```

Word Bank

bee	bird	bull	cat	cow	wife
dog	farmer	goat	goose	mule	

Name _____ Date _____

JOHN SCIESZKA

<u>The True Story of the 3 Little Pigs</u>

Read *The True Story of the 3 Little Pigs* by A. Wolf. I'm not sure how reliable this A. Wolf is. His version of the story is very different than the one I know. What do you think? If he tells a different side of this story, what do you think about the *The Tale of Little Red Riding Hood*? What do you think he would change about that story? Use the lines below to write events from *The Tale of Little Red Riding Hood* and how the wolf might change them.

Version We Know   **Wolf's Side of the Story**

_____   _____

_____   _____

_____   _____

_____   _____

_____   _____

_____   _____

_____   _____

For other 3 Little Pig Stories try:
The Three Little Pigs by Margot Zemach (Farrar, Straus, Giroux, 1988)
The Three Pigs by Tony Ross (Pantheon, 1983)

Name _____   **Date** _____

MICHAEL HAGUE
Alphabears

 Read *Alphabears*. Michael drew the pictures for his wife Kathleen's story about bears. They both love bears. Write a story about your own favorite animal, such as Alphacats, Alphadinos, or Alphasnakes. Draw your own pictures or work with a friend who draws well. Write your story in rhyme as Kathleen did or write it without rhymes. Use the lines below to begin your rough draft.

_____
title
_____
_____
_____
_____
_____
_____
_____
_____
_____

Name _____ **Date** _____

ANTHONY BROWNE

Willy the Wimp

Read *Willy The Wimp*. Willy learns that muscles aren't the answer to his problem. But muscles are an important part of our body. Do research in your media center about muscles. Use an encyclopedia or a book about our muscular system.

Every great report starts with an outline. Use these questions to guide your research. After you answer these questions, you will be on your way to writing a great report.

Questions to guide research on muscles

1. What are muscles?

2. Why are muscles important? What do they do?

3. Are there different kinds of muscles? Do they have different jobs to do?

4. What makes some muscles ill? Are there diseases that only attack muscles?

Use the following lines to write other questions that you would like to answer about muscles.

_____

_____

_____

_____

_____

Name _____ Date _____

DIANE GOODE

I Hear a Noise

Read *I Hear a Noise*. Diane wrote a story about a little girl who really did hear a noise before she fell asleep. What a surprise ending! That oh-so-very-big monster turned out to be a very small monster. Write your own "Noise" story with a surprise ending. Use the lines below to begin your rough draft.

_____
title

_____

_____

_____

_____

_____

_____

_____

_____

_____

Name _____ **Date** _____

JOHN STEPTOE

Mufaro's Beautiful Daughters

Read *Mufaro's Beautiful Daughters*. This beautiful African fairy tale is very similar to Cinderella. Like Cinderella, the beautiful Nyasha overcomes the evil plan of her sister Manyara to live happily ever after.

Here are three activities you can do with this story. Pick the one you want to do after you have read the book.

1. Rewrite the story of *Mufaro's Beautiful Daughters* or Cinderella in your own words. Draw pictures to go with your story.

2. Write your own fairy tale about a beautiful girl who overcomes evil by being as good as she can be. Read *Snow White in New York* by Fiona French (Oxford University Press, 1986) for inspiration.

3. Write your own fairy tale about a handsome prince who overcomes his evil twin brother. The evil twin is two minutes younger than the handsome prince. He is not next in line for the throne. But when the goodly king dies, the evil twin takes the throne from his kind brother. How can you (as the author) put the handsome prince back on his throne?
Remember: the handsome prince hates war and killing. He will need to be tricky to get his throne back.

Name _____   Date _____

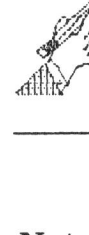

TOMIE DEPAOLA

The Legend of the Indian Paintbrush

Notes to the teacher:

1. Read *The Legend of the Indian Paintbrush* to your students.

2. This beautiful tale from the Southwest is the story behind a flower. Find pictures to bring to class to show the children.

3. Assemble mural paper (butcher or bulletin board) and watercolors.

4. Help the children retell the important parts of the story.

5. Help the children reproduce the paintings from DePaola's beautiful book. They can focus on plants, landscape, sunrise, sunset, or Indian artifacts.

6. Invite other classes into your room so that your children can retell the story to them.

7. Lend the mural to other classes so they may enjoy it for several days or a week. This is called "A Traveling Story Wall." Children from younger grades enjoy the traveling story wall because they can see one of the exciting activities waiting for them in the upper grades. Older children also enjoy seeing the work of younger students.

Name _____   Date _____

DONALD HALL

The Ox-Cart Man

Notes to the teacher:

1. Have the students read *The Ox-Cart Man*. Barbara Cooney won the Caldecott Award for her pictures in this story told by Donald Hall. We can see in the pictures and hear in the story how different life was in the early 1800s.

2. Arrange children in groups for research. Have the children brainstorm questions for research. Assemble books and encyclopedias on these topics or send them to the media center. Sample topics include:
   —Shearing sheep and how yarn is made from the wool
   —Making candles
   —Making maple syrup

3. *Assign the project*: Write a how-to-do book on a topic. Include pictures.

4. Discuss the concept behind a how-to-do book. Bring in examples from the media center. Aliki's *How a Book Is Made* is a good example. Other possibilities are how-to handicraft books.

5. Have the students write key questions about their topic to guide their research. For other ideas, they can ask classmates what they would like to know about the topic.

Name _____ Date _____

HANS WILHELM

I'll Always Love You

Read *I'll Always Love You*. This is a happy, tender, and sad story. It shows all the different sides of life. The important message from Hans is that everything and everyone we love should know how we feel. If you love someone, let that person know.

Write and illustrate your own book for someone you love. Let that person know why and how you love him or her. It could be mom, dad, grandma, grandpa, aunt, uncle, brother, sister, teacher, principal, bus driver, or any special person you know. Use the lines below to write a rough draft of ideas about the way you love that person.

_____

_____

_____

_____

_____

_____

_____

_____

Name _____ **Date** _____

TARO YASHIMA
The Umbrella

Read *The Umbrella*. Write about your favorite part of the story in the umbrella shape.

Name _____ **Date** _____

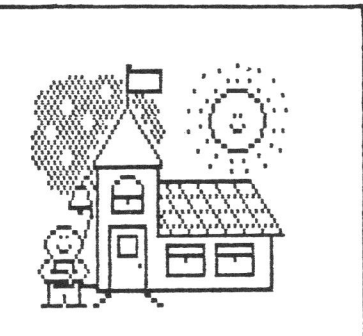

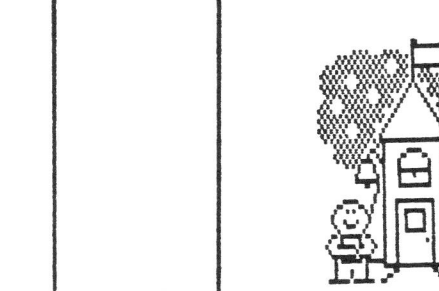

☆ Bernard Most
☆ Syd Hoff
☆ Else Holmelund
☆ H. A. Rey
☆ Bernard Waber
☆ Diane Goode
☆ Anthony Browne
☆ Demi

September
Primary I

☆ Aliki
☆ Jack Prelutsky
☆ Tomie de Paola
☆ Stan Berenstain
☆ Taro Yashima
☆ Michael Hague
☆ Hans Wilhelm

September
Primary II

☆ Alfred Slote
☆ Roald Dahl
☆ Robert McCloskey
☆ Paul Goble
☆ Edgar d' Aulaire

September
Intermediate

SEPTEMBER ANSWER KEY

Aliki Brandenberg: *Digging Up Dinosaurs*

1. Dinosaur dies and ends up in a body of water.
2. Bones are covered by mud.
3. Mud and bones turn to stone.
4. Dinosaur is not seen for millions of years.
5. Earth is weathered away.
6. A part of the dinosaur bone is discovered.

Byron Barton: *Buzz, Buzz, Buzz*

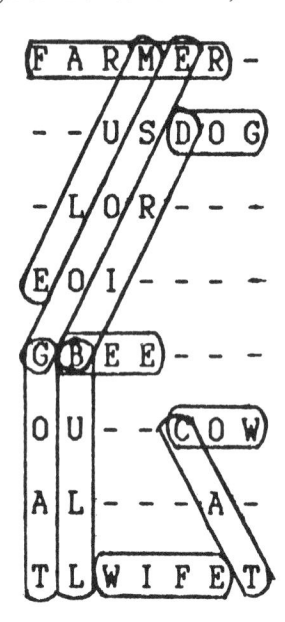

```
F A R M E R - -
- - U S D O G -
- L O R - - - -
E O I - - - - -
G B E E - - - -
O U - - C O W -
A L - - - A - -
T L W I F E T -
```

SEPTEMBER AUTHORS BIBLIOGRAPHY

September   Demi (Demi Hitz)

Demi's Find the Animals ABC (Putnam, 1985); *Dragon Kites and Dragonflies: A Collection of Chinese Nursery Rhymes* (HBJ, 1986); *A Chinese Zoo: Fables and Proverbs* (HBJ, 1987); *Demi's Reflective Fables* (Putnam, 1988).

September 3   Aliki Brandenberg

Keep Your Mouth Closed, Dear (Dial, 1966); *Mummies Made in Egypt* (Harper, 1979); *Digging Up Dinosaurs* (Crowell, 1981); *At Mary Bloom's* (Greenwillow, 1983); *Wild and Woolly Mammoths* (Harper, 1983); *Feelings* (Greenwillow, 1984); *Dinosaurs Are Different* (Crowell, 1985); *My Visit to the Dinosaurs* (Harper, 1985); *How a Book Is Made* (Harper, 1986); *Digging Up Dinosaurs* (Harper, 1988, revised).

September 8   Byron Barton

Elephant (Houghton Mifflin, 1971); *Hester* (Penguin, 1978); *Airplanes, Airports, Trains, Trucks, and Wheels* (Crowell, 1984); *Building a House* (Penguin, 1984); *If You Were an Astronaut* (Penguin, 1991).

September 8   John Scieszka (and Alexander Wolf)

The True Story of the 3 Little Pigs (Viking, 1989); *The Frog Prince Continued* (Viking, 1991).

September 8   Michael Hague (as illustrator)

Demetrius and the Golden Goblet (HBJ, 1980); *East of the Sun, West of the Moon* (HBJ, 1980); *The Dragon Kite* (HBJ, 1982); *Alphabears* (Holt, 1985); *Numbears* (Holt, 1986); *World of the Unicorns* (Holt, 1986).

September 11   Anthony Browne

Gorilla (Knopf, 1985); *Piggybook* (Knopf, 1986); *Willy the Champ* (Knopf, 1986); *Look What I've Got* (Knopf, 1988); *Things I Like* (Knopf, 1989).

September 14   Diane Goode

My Little Library of Christmas Classics, illustrator (Random, 1983); *When I Was Young in the Mountains*, illustrator (Dutton, 1985); *Watch the Stars Come Out*, illustrator (Dutton, 1986); *I Hear a Noise*, author/illustrator (Dutton, 1989).

September 14   John Steptoe

Stevie (Harper, 1969); *Baby Says* (Lothrop, 1988); *The Story of Jumping Mouse* (Morrow, 1989).

September 15 Tomie de Paola

Strega Nona (Prentice-Hall, 1975)—1976 Caldecott Honor Book; *Pancakes for Breakfast* (HBJ, 1978); *The Lady of Guadalupe* (Holiday, 1980); *The Legend of the Bluebonnet* (Putnam, 1983); *Mysterious Giant of Barletta* (HBJ, 1984); *Merry Christmas, Strega Nona* (HBJ, 1986); *Strega Nona's Magic Lessons* (HBJ, 1986).

September 20 Donald Hall

The Ox-Cart Man (Viking, 1979)—1980 Caldecott Award Winner.

September 21 Hans Wilhelm

Tales from the Land Under My Table (Random, 1983); *A New Home, a New Friend* (Random, 1985); *Pirates, Ahoy* (Parents, 1987); *Oh, What a Mess* (Crown, 1988); *Tyrone the Horrible* (Scholastic, 1988).

September 21 Taro Yashima

Crow Boy (Viking, 1955)—1956 Caldecott Honor Book; *Momo's Kitten* (Penguin, 1977); *Umbrella* (Penguin, 1977).

OCTOBER

October 2	Reeve Lindbergh, *Midnight Farm*, illustrated by Susan Jeffers (October 7) (writing letters)
October 3	John Himmelman, *Amanda and the Witch Switch* (you're the witch activity)
October 8	Edward Ormondroyd, *Broderick* (story comparisons)
October 9	Karen Ackerman, *Song and Dance Man* (interviewing grandparents)
October 10	Robert D. San Souci, *The Legend of Scarface* (writing a legend)* Robert D. San Souci, *The Talking Eggs* (making comparisons)*
October 14	Polly Cameron, *I Can't Said the Ant* (writing rhymes)
October 20	Lulu Delacre, *Arroz Con Leche* (speaking Spanish)*
October 21	Janet Ahlberg, *The Jolly Postman* (writing dialogues)
October 25	Paula Winter, *The Bear & the Fly* (writing a story)
October 31	Cyndy Szekeres, *Moving Day* ("what if" writing game)

October Bookmarks
October Answer Key
October Authors Bibliography

*Denotes multicultural title/activity

OCTOBER AUTHORS

DATE	NAME	AUTHOR/ILLUSTRATOR		READING LEVEL			
				K	1	2	3
2	Reeve Lindbergh	X		X	X	X	
3	John Himmelman	X	X	X	X	X	
6	Steven Kellogg	X	X	X	X	X	
7	Susan Jeffers		X				
7	Alice Dalgliesh	X				X	X
8	Edward Ormondroyd	X				X	X
9	Karen Ackerman	X		X	X	X	X
9	Johanna Hurwitz	X				X	X
10	Robert San Souci	X		X	X	X	X
10	James Marshall	X	X	X	X	X	X
10	Nancy Carlson	X	X	X	X	X	
14	Miriam Cohen	X		X	X	X	
14	Polly Cameron	X		X	X	X	
16	Noah Webster	Lexicographer					
19	Ed Emberley		X				
20	Crockett Johnson	X	X	X	X	X	
20	Lulu Delacre	X		X	X	X	
21	Janet Ahlberg	X	X	X	X	X	
24	Bruno Munari	X	X	X	X	X	
25	Paula Winter	X	X	X	X		
28	Leonard Kessler	X	X		X	X	
31	Cyndy Szekeres	X	X	X	X	X	

REEVE LINDBERGH/SUSAN JEFFERS

<u>Midnight Farm</u>

Read *Midnight Farm*. This book was written and illustrated by two ladies born in October. Reeve Lindbergh, born on October 2, wrote the story and Susan Jeffers, born on October 7, illustrated it. Reeve and Susan love to write and draw. Susan's favorite animal is the horse. Can you tell?

Susan works very hard at her craft. Select two pictures from the story. Write several sentences about each picture explaining why you like them. Send Susan a note telling her what a wonderful artist she is. Write Reeve a letter telling her how much you liked her story. Here is an address you can use to write to them.

> Susan Jeffers or Reeve Lindbergh
> c/o Dial Books for Young Readers
> 2 Park Avenue
> New York, NY 10016

Picture 1 _____

_____

_____

_____

Picture 2 _____

_____

_____

_____

Name _____ Date _____

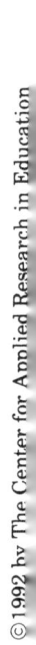

JOHN HIMMELMAN

Amanda and the Witch Switch

Read *Amanda and the Witch Switch*. Amanda makes a mistake when she changes the frog into a wizard. But the wizard learns his lesson in the end. What three wishes would you make if Amanda turned you into a witch or wizard? Use the lines below to explain your wishes.

_____

_____

_____

_____

_____

_____

_____

Name _____   Date _____

EDWARD ORMONDROYD

Broderick

Read *Broderick*. What an exciting life Broderick had. All that excitement was inspired by a story. Reading can have a strong effect on our lives.

Edward Ormondroyd suggests that we read *Norman the Doorman* by Don Freeman. Do that! Then compare the two stories. How are they alike? How are they different? Use the lines below for your answers.

_____

_____

_____

_____

_____

_____

_____

Name _____ Date _____

KAREN ACKERMAN

Song and Dance Man

Read *Song and Dance Man*. Karen Ackerman wrote this 1989 Caldecott Award book. Stephen Gammell created the winning illustrations with colored pencil. This story is a glimpse of the past a grandfather gives to his grandchildren. Interview your grandfather or grandmother and write a story from their past.

1. What job did they have? _____

_____

_____

2. What did they like about it best? _____

_____

_____

3. What did they like least? _____

_____

_____

4. What is their favorite thing to do when the television and radio are off?

_____

_____

_____

Name _____   Date _____

ROBERT D. SAN SOUCI

The Legend of Scarface

Read *The Legend of Scarface*. This legend is a story told by the Blackfeet Indians. Go to the media center and find a book or encyclopedia that has other Indian legends in it. Try to find other Blackfeet legends. Use the lines below to collect notes on the important parts of the legend or legends you read.

Tell one or more legends in your own words. This is called retelling a tale. Robert San Souci did it and you can, too—even though his brother Robert won't be able to draw your illustrations for you!

Place your story with other stories from your class in a binder or folder. You will then have a collection of Indian legends to check out from your room.

_____

_____

_____

_____

_____

_____

_____

_____

_____

Name _____ **Date** _____

ROBERT D. SAN SOUCI

The Talking Eggs

Read *The Talking Eggs*. This legend is very similar to *Cinderella*. *Cinderella* is a French tale and *The Talking Eggs* is an adaptation of a story from the Creole region of the American South. How can that be?

Investigate Creole in a book from your media center and discover what it means. Then compare *Cinderella* and *The Talking Eggs* using the lines below.

Cinderella   **The Talking Eggs**

1. Who was nice?

2. Who was mean?

3. Who worked the magic?

4. What was similar about the gifts?

5. How were the endings different? This will depend on the version of Cinderella you use. Try *Cinderella* retold by Amy Ehrlich and illustrated by Susan Jeffers (Dial, 1985). Use the back of this sheet for longer answers.

Name _____   Date _____

POLLY CAMERON

I Can't Said the Ant

Read *I Can't Said the Ant*. Polly told her story in rhyme just like the following examples. Write rhyming quotations on the lines below and draw a picture in the frames to go with them. Here are some examples:

"I love to rhyme," said the lime.
"Me too," said the stew.

Try using the names of the people in your classroom:

"Up the hill," said Bill.
"Don't get in a stew," said Andrew.
"I will," said Bill.
"That's not fair," said Clare.
"Oh gee!" said Stephanie.

Name _____   Date _____

LULU DELACRE

Arroz Con Leche

NOTE TO TEACHER: Read *Arroz Con Leche*. Sharing a foreign language with children is like showing them the keys to a new world. Children are fascinated that other sounds can actually mean something. If you have any Spanish language in your background, this activity will be fun for you as well as for the children. Read several poems and teach the children a little about pronunciation so they can read with you.

If you have no Spanish language in your background, ask the other teachers in your building. If no one knows any Spanish, go to the bookstore and purchase one of the inexpensive foreign language phrase books. They have a pronunciation guide in the front. I recommend *Charles Berlitz Passport to Spanish* from Signet.

Practice some of the phrases. Make them silly. Examples: Tengo un dolor de muela; I have a toothache. When you think you have a nice Spanish accent, practice several of the poems.

On the day you intend to read the poems, start talking to the children in the Spanish phrases you practiced. Pretend that you all know Spanish. You won't believe the looks you will get. Then speak in English and say, "Oh. I've been reading this wonderful book of songs and poems in Spanish and I must have forgotten where I was. Would you like to hear some?" The response will be overwhelming!

Ask your music teacher to record the sheet music for the songs at the back of the book. Have a Spanish sing along.

Enjoy *Arroz Con Leche* and the joy of bringing a foreign language to the ears of your children. If any of your students speak Spanish at home— you're lucky to have a resident expert!

P. S. Here is another excellent title: *Tortillas Pour Mama: and other Nursery Rhymes/Spanish and English* by Margot C. Griego et al, illustrated by Barbara Cooney (Holt, 1981).

JANET AHLBERG

The Jolly Postman or Other People's Letters

Read *The Jolly Postman or Other People's Letters*. This story is a collection of letters from one character in a story to another character. Since all these characters are writing letters, we should too!

Here are activities for *The Jolly Postman*. Do one, all, or as many as you like.

1. Write a letter to Goldilocks as little bear would reply to the invitation to her party.

2. If you were the witch from the gingerbread house, what would you order from the witch catalog that came in the mail? Fill out an order blank and give the prices.

3. Write a reply as the wolf to Harold Meeny.

4. Write a dialogue between two characters of one book or two characters who are not in the same book.

Example: One of the Three Pigs meets Peter Pumpkin Eater

The pig from the brick house meets Peter Pumpkin Eater, who kept his wife in a pumpkin shell. What would the pig smart enough to build a brick home say to the silly Peter Pumpkin Eater?

Name _____ Date _____

PAULA WINTER
The Bear & the Fly

Read *The Bear & the Fly*. This story has no words, but you can still "read" the pictures. As you read the pictures, write the story you hear happening in your mind. Write your story on 3" × 5" self-stick removeable notes and attach them to the correct pages. Let someone in your class read the story.

There are other illustrators who DRAW books for you to read also. You might like to see them.

Lena Anderson: *Bunny Bath; Bunny Box; Bunny Fun; Bunny Party; Bunny Story; Bunny Surprise* (all available from Farrar

Alan Baker: *Benjamin's Box* (out of print, but may be on library shelves)

Raymond Briggs: *The Snowman* (Random, 1988); *Father Christmas* (Putnam, 1973)

Peter Collington: *The Angel and the Soldier Boy* (Knopf, 1987); *On Christmas Eve* (Knopf, 1990)

Alexandra Day: *Good Dog, Carl* (Green Tiger Press, 1985); *Carl Goes Shopping* (Farrar, 1989); *Carl's Christmas* (Farrar, 1989); *Frank and Ernest* (Scholastic, 1988)

Pat Hutchins: *Changes, Changes* (Macmillan, 1987)

Fernando Krahn: *Amanda and the Mysterious Carpet* (Houghton, 1985); *Arthur's Adventure in the Abandoned House* (Dutton, 1981); *How Santa Had a Long and Difficult Journey* (Dell, 1988); *Mystery of the Giant's Footprints* (Dutton, 1977); *Robot-Bot-Bot* (Dutton, 1979); *Secret in the Dungeon* (Houghton, 1983)

Mercer Mayer: *Oops; Ah-Choo; Hiccup; A Boy, a Dog, and a Frog* (there are many books about the small boy and his frog in this series available from Dial Books)

Dieter Schubert: *Where's My Monkey?* (Dial, 1987)

David Wiesner: *Free Fall* (Lothrop, 1988); *Tuesday* (Lothrop, 1990). Although not totally wordless, they offer an opportunity to create a story line.

CYNDY SZEKERES

Moving Day

Read *Moving Day*. Let's play one of my favorite writing games. "What if . . ."

In this game, a reader becomes a writer and changes the ending of the story. We can add different problems to Cyndy's story. She chose to write one story, but there are more problems a mouse family could have on a moving day. All goes well with the mouse family on moving day. But how would the story have ended if . . .

Choose one of the new problems below, and write a new ending on your own paper. OR make up your own problem ending for the mouse family.

1. Late the first night, a snake comes back to HIS home under the pine tree roots. What does he say? What does he do? What would the poor mouse family say and do?

2. Early the next morning, a baby kitten crawls out of the back of the dry little cave. She is lost. She is hungry. What will the mouse family do?

3. Late the next afternoon, another mouse family comes back from a vacation to claim their home. Mr. Mole was supposed to watch their house, but after he left, somebody took all their furniture. Now there's a problem!

Name _____ **Date** _____

October Primary I

- Robert Lawson
- Polly Cameron
- Edward Ormondroyd
- James Marshall
- Susan Jeffers (illustrator)
- John Himmelman
- Karen Ackerman
- Cyndy Szekeres

October Primary II

- Steven Kellogg
- Nancy Carlson
- Crockett Johnson
- Leonard Kessler
- Miriam Cohen
- Reeve Lindbergh
- Robert San Souci
- Janet Ahlberg

October Intermediate

- Robert Lawson
- Natalie Savage Carlson
- Donald Sobol
- Johanna Hurwitz
- Ed Emberley (illustrator)
- Molly Cone
- Lois Lenski

OCTOBER ANSWER KEY

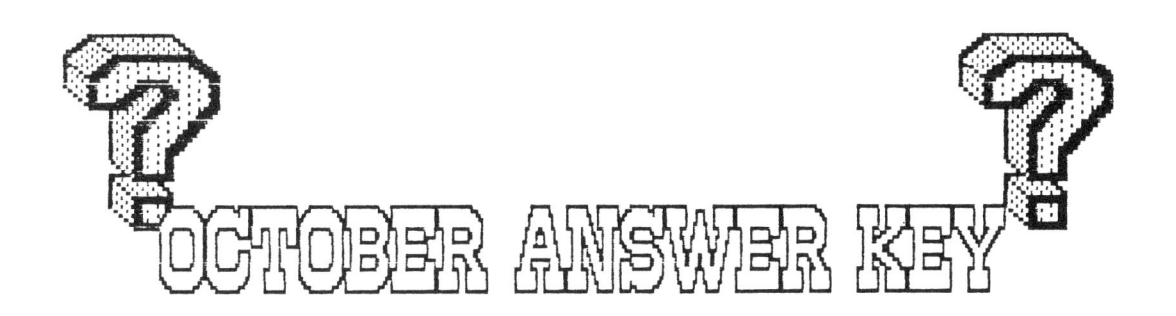

Edward Ormondroyd: *Broderick*

    a. *Broderick* and Don Freeman's *Norman the Doorman* are the same—mice, have jobs, become famous with real people.

    b. *Broderick* and *Norman the Doorman* are different—Norman was a doorman, loved art, was a painter, won an art contest. Broderick ate books, was a great surfer, had a film about him, gave lectures.

Robert D. San Souci: *The Legend of Scarface*

The critical parts of a legend:

    a. set in a specific historical time and place

    b. characters are people, animals have human qualities, gods have supernatural powers

    c. presents a story explaining why something exists or how something came to exist

Robert D. San Souci: *The Talking Eggs*

Creole comes from the Spanish word *criollo*, meaning "native to the place." This refers to the French and Spanish settlers of the area.

1. Cinderella; Blanche
2. Stepmother and stepsisters; Rose and the mother
3. Fairy godmother; old woman in the woods
4. Pretty clothes and a carriage
5. Cinderella gave her sisters a room to live in in the castle and fine gentlemen to marry them. Rose and her mother wander the rest of their days looking for the old woman's house.

OCTOBER AUTHORS BIBLIOGRAPHY

October 2 Reeve Lindbergh
Midnight Farm (Dial, 1987); *Benjamin's Barn* (Dial, 1989)

October 3 John Himmelman
The Talking Tree (Penguin, 1986); *Amanda and the Magic Garden* (Penguin, 1987); *Montigue on the High Seas* (Penguin, 1988)

October 7 Susan Jeffers (illustrator)
Three Jovial Huntsmen (Bradbury, 1973)—1974 Caldecott Honor Book; *Wild Robin* (Dutton, 1976); *Hansel and Gretel* (Dial, 1980); *Snow Queen* (Dial, 1982); *Silent Night* (Dutton, 1984); *All the Pretty Horses* (Scholastic, 1985); *Midnight Farm* by Reeve Lindbergh (Dial, 1987)

October 8 Edward Ormondroyd
Theodore (Houghton, 1984); *Johnny Castleseed* (Houghton, 1985); *Theodore's Rival* (Houghton, 1986)

October 9 Karen Ackerman
Song and Dance Man (Knopf, 1988)—1989 Caldecott Award Book

October 10 Robert D. San Souci
Legend of Sleepy Hollow (Doubleday, 1986); *The Enchanted Tapestry* (Dial, 1987); *Short and Shivery: Thirty Chilling Tales* (Doubleday, 1987); *Six Swans* (Simon & Schuster, 1989); *The Talking Eggs* (Dial, 1989); *The White Cat* (Orchard, 1989); *Young Merlin* (Doubleday, 1990)

October 14 Polly Cameron
I Can't Said the Ant (Scholastic, 1961)

October 20 Lulu Delacre
Lullabies (Simon & Schuster, 1984); *Nathan and Nicholas Alexander* (Scholastic, 1986); *Nathan's Fishing Trip* (Scholastic, 1988)

October 21 Janet Ahlberg
Ha Ha Bonk Bonk Bonk (Penguin, 1982); *Peek-a-Boo* (Penguin, 1984); *Each Peach Pear Plum* (Penguin, 1986); *The Jolly Postman or Other People's Letters* (Little, 1986)

October 24 Paula Winter
The Bear & the Fly (Crown, 1987)

October 31 Cyndy Szekeres
All published by Western Publishing: *Favorite Two-Minute Stories* (1987); *Counting Book 1 to 10* (1987); *Good Night, Sweet Mouse* (1988); *The New Baby* (1989); *A Fine Mouse Band* (1989); *A Busy Day* (1989); *Moving Day* (1989)

NOVEMBER

November 4	Gail Haley, *A Story, A Story* (writing activity)*
November 9	Lois Ehlert, *Eating the Alphabet:* Fruits and Vegetables from A to Z (writing activity)
November 13	Nathaniel Benchley, *The Strange Disappearance of Arthur Cluck* (fill in)
November 14	Alan Baker, *Benjamin's Portrait* (portraiture)
November 16	Jean Fritz, *Who's That Stepping on Plymouth Rock?* (personal museum)
November 19	Margaret Musgrove, *Ashanti to Zulu* (ABC book)*
November 19	Ann H. Scott, *Sam* (writing activity)*
November 20	William Cole, *Poem Stew* (gathering poems)
November 27	Kevin Henkes, *Once Around the Block*, illustrated by Victoria Chess (November 16) (writing/mapping/drawing)
November 28	Ed Young, *Lon Po Po* (comparisons)*
November 28	Stephanie Calmenson, *The Principal's New Clothes* (writing activity)

November Bookmarks
November Answer Key
November Authors Bibliography

*Denotes multicultural title/activity

NOVEMBER AUTHORS

DATE	NAME	AUTHOR	ILLUSTRATOR	K	1	2	3
4	Gail Haley	X	X				
8	Marianna Mayer	X	X			X	X
9	Lois Ehlert	X	X	X	X	X	
10	Kate Seredy	X	X	X	X		
12	Marjorie Sharmat	X		X	X	X	
13	Nathaniel Benchley	X		X	X	X	
14	Astrid Lindgren	X		X	X	X	
14	Alan Baker	X	X	X	X		
14	Miska Miles	X				X	X
15	Daniel Pinkwater	X				X	X
16	Jean Fritz	X					X
16	Victoria Chess		X	X	X	X	
19	Margaret Musgrove	X				X	X
19	Ann H. Scott	X		X	X	X	
20	William Cole	editor of poetry				X	X
23	Marc Simont		X				
24	Carlo Collodi	X					X
24	Mordicai Gerstein	X	X			X	X
25	Marc Brown	X	X	X	X	X	
26	Charles Schulz	X	X	Everyone loves Peanuts!			
27	Kevin Henkes	X		X	X		
28	Ed Young	X	X	X	X	X	
28	Stephanie Calmenson	X			X	X	
28	Tomi Ungerer	X	X		X	X	
30	Margot Zemach	X	X		X	X	

GAIL HALEY

A Story, a Story

Read *A Story, A Story*. Use the words in the Word Bank to fill in these sentences about tricky Ananse, the Spider Man.

1. Ananse wanted _____ from the Sky God.

2. Ananse had to catch a spotted _____ with terrible _____.

3. Ananse also caught _____ that stung like fire.

4. Ananse tricked the _____ people who cannot see.

5. The little wooden doll was covered with _____ gum.

6. Ananse _____ a web up to the Sky God.

7. The Sky God gave Ananse a _____ box full of stories.

8. Ananse stories started in _____.

9. Ananse was small, but he was very _____.

Word Bank

Africa	fairy	golden	hornets	leopard
smart	spun	sticky	stories	teeth

Name _____ Date _____

LOIS EHLERT

Eating the Alphabet

Read *Eating the Alphabet: Fruits and Vegetables from A to Z.* Lois loves bright colors and fruits and veggies. She could have written an alphabet book about things in a house, a school, or things to be thankful for.

Pick a topic and write your own alphabet book. Use the lines below to write ideas for the letters you will use in your alphabet book.

Alphabet Book About _____

_____

_____

_____

_____

_____

_____

_____

_____

Name _____ **Date** _____

NATHANIEL BENCHLEY

The Strange Disappearance of Arthur Cluck

Read *The Strange Disappearance of Arthur Cluck*. Use the words in the Word Bank to fill in these sentences.

1. Arthur was a young _____.

2. Arthur rode on his mother's _____.

3. One morning, Arthur was _____.

4. Arthur's mother asked the _____ in the pond. But he didn't know.

5. She asked the _____. But he was too busy crowing.

6. The cow sent her to the _____.

7. The owl jumped on the _____.

8. The rat had _____ eggs.

9. There were many chickens in the _____.

10. Only the real Arthur could _____ on the owl's head.

Word Bank

chicken	colored	duck	fox	gone
head	owl	ride	rooster	truck

Name _____ Date _____

ALAN BAKER
Benjamin's Portrait

Read *Benjamin's Portrait*. Talented hamsters like Benjamin are very rare. But talented children are all over America and the world. Benjamin solved his portrait problem by deciding to photograph himself. Why don't you try a self-portrait? Here are a number of ways for you to do it. Pick one and get started.

1. Use watercolors, tempera, pastel chalks, or oil paints to paint your portrait.

2. Take a picture of yourself with a camera. There are several ways. Figure them out. Or have a friend take your picture.

3. Use a video camera to make a video portrait. Make a video of you doing your favorite activity.

Name _____   Date _____

JEAN FRITZ

Who's That Stepping on Plymouth Rock?

Read *Who's That Stepping on Plymouth Rock?* Many people had a difficult time saving the rock that marked the place of the Pilgrims' landing. There are many important things in your life, too. Answer the questions below to help you create a museum display for an important symbol or thing in your life.

1. Do you have a special thing that you really love? What is it?
   _____

2. If you were to save this thing for a long time, to share with your grandchildren, how would you preserve it?
   _____
   _____
   _____

3. Make a model (either on paper or with real materials) to display your important thing.

4. Pretend you are the curator of your museum display. Write a speech to explain why your thing is important to you.

5. Present your speech to your class.

Name _____ Date _____

MARGARET MUSGROVE

Ashanti to Zulu

Read *Ashanti to Zulu*. Margaret wrote an alphabet book about the culture of African countries. There are many countries and topics that need alphabet books written about them. Select one of the ideas below and write an alphabet book. Be sure to illustrate it.

1. Pick a country in the world or a state in America and write an alphabet book about the important ideas of the country and state.

2. Write an alphabet book about you, your teacher, classmates, and school.

3. Write an alphabet book about the country of your ancestors.

4. Write an alphabet book about your favorite hobby, sport, or activity.

Name _____   Date _____

ANN H. SCOTT
Sam

Read *Sam*. Ann Scott wrote a very touching story about a little boy who has nothing to do and no one to play with. Everyone else has something to do. Many families are busy today. Write a letter to Sam and tell him the things you do when everyone is too busy to play with you.

_____

_____

_____

_____

_____

_____

_____

_____

_____

Name _____ **Date** _____

WILLIAM COLE
Poem Stew

NOTE TO THE TEACHER: Read many of the great poems in *Poem Stew* to your students. William Cole is the editor of many funny volumes of poetry. As editor, he finds his favorite poems and puts them into one book that a publisher accepts and publishes.

ACTIVITY FOR THE CHILDREN: Have the students find and neatly print three of their favorite poems and draw pictures to go with them. Have them put one poem on each piece of paper. Everyone in the classroom will do this activity so that they will publish their own *Poem Stew*.

Display as many of these books as you have so the children can make their selections. Other poetry books are also suitable.

Bear Hugs by Kathleen & Michael Hague (Henry Holt, 1989)
Beastly Boys and Ghastly Girls edited by William Cole (Dell, 1977)
Beneath a Blue Umbrella by Jack Prelutsky (Greenwillow, 1990)
The Book of Pigericks by Arnold Lobel (Harper, 1983)
The Butterfly Jar by Jeff Moss (Bantam, 1989)
Dirty Beasts by Roald Dahl (Puffin Books, 1983)
For Laughing Out Loud selected by Jack Prelutsky (Knopf, 1991)
Hailstones and Halibut Bones by Mary O'Neill (Doubleday, 1989 rev.)
The Headless Horseman Rides Tonight by Jack Prelutsky (Greenwillow, 1980)
If I Were in Charge of the World and Other Worries by Judith Viorst (Macmillan, 1981)
It's Christmas by Jack Prelutsky (Greenwillow, 1981)
It's Thanksgiving by Jack Prelutsky (Greenwillow, 1982)
A Light in the Attic by Shel Silverstein (Harper, 1981)
Monster Knock-Knocks by William Cole (Simon & Schuster, 1988)
The New Kid on the Block by Jack Prelutsky (Greenwillow, 1984)
Nightmares: Poems to Trouble Your Sleep by Jack Prelutsky (Greenwillow, 1976)
Oh, Such Foolishness by William Cole (Harper, 1978)
Oh, That's Ridiculous by William Cole (Penguin, 1988)
Random House Book of Poetry for Children edited by Jack Prelutsky (Random House, 1983)
Red Is My Favorite Color by Phyllis Halloran (Reading Inc., 1988)
Ride a Purple Pelican by Jack Prelutsky (Greenwillow, 1986)
Sing a Song of Popcorn selected by Beatrice Schenck DeRegniers and others (Scholastic, 1988)
Something Big Has Been Here by Jack Prelutsky (Greenwillow, 1990)
Where the Sidewalk Ends by Shel Silverstein (Harper, 1974)
Whiskers and Rhymes by Arnold Lobel (Greenwillow, 1985)
Zoo Doings: Animal Poems by Jack Prelutsky (Greenwillow, 1983)

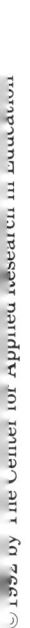

KEVIN HENKES/VICTORIA CHESS

Once Around the Block

Read *Once Around the Block*. Both the author Kevin and the illustrator Victoria were born in November. They worked very well together on this book. Let's see how well you can cooperate with a classmate. Pick a partner and do the following activity.

Write a story about your imaginary block. Use ideas about your neighbors and your partner's neighbors.

Draw a map of your pretend block. Show where the neighbors live. Include pictures of your neighbors doing the things they like most.

What do they do in their yards?

What do they do for you that makes you like them?

List other important ideas you need to think about before you begin.

_____

_____

_____

_____

_____

_____

_____

Name _____ Date _____

ED YOUNG

Lon Po Po

Read *Lon Po Po*. Ed Young won the Caldecott Award for writing and drawing the pictures for this fairy tale from China. It sounds like Little Red Riding Hood, doesn't it? Let's compare Ed's story with the story of Little Red Riding Hood we all know. Answer these questions.

Lon Po Po	*Little Red Riding Hood*
1. Number of children in this story:	
2. Advice mother gave:	
3. Who went to grandma's house?	
4. Who did the wolf pretend to be?	
5. How were the endings different?	

Name _____ Date _____

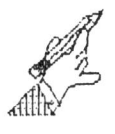

STEPHANIE CALMENSON

The Principal's New Clothes

Read *The Principal's New Clothes*. This take-off on *The Emperor's New Clothes* is the perfect chance for you to show how well you can write.

Follow this outline to help you begin.

1. Introduce the main character, who must be a vain person (could be a lady) concerned about his or her clothes; for example, president, mailman, restaurant owner.

2. Describe in several scenes how vain that person is.

3. Introduce the tricky people who will make the most beautiful cloth.

4. They meet the main character and convince him or her that he or she must have this cloth.

5. Everyone is suspicious of how the cloth is coming along. The tricky people explain only fools cannot see the cloth.

6. The great day comes and the vain person makes his or her appearance in nothing but his or her underwear.

7. The end of the story happens when an honest child exclaims:

    "I can see underwear!" Who will it be?

8. The main character rewards the honest child. What will the reward be?

Name _____ Date _____

Gail Haley
Marianna Mayer
William Steig
Marc Brown
Kevin Henkes
Ann Scott
Stephanie Calmenson

November
Primary I

Marjorie Sharmat
Nathaniel Benchley
Leo Politi
Tomi Ungerer
Margaret Musgrove
Ed Young
Astrid Lindgren

November
Primary II

Miska Miles
Jean Fritz
William Steig
Charles Schulz
Daniel Pinkwater
William Cole
Astrid Lindgren

November
Intermediate

NOVEMBER ANSWER KEY

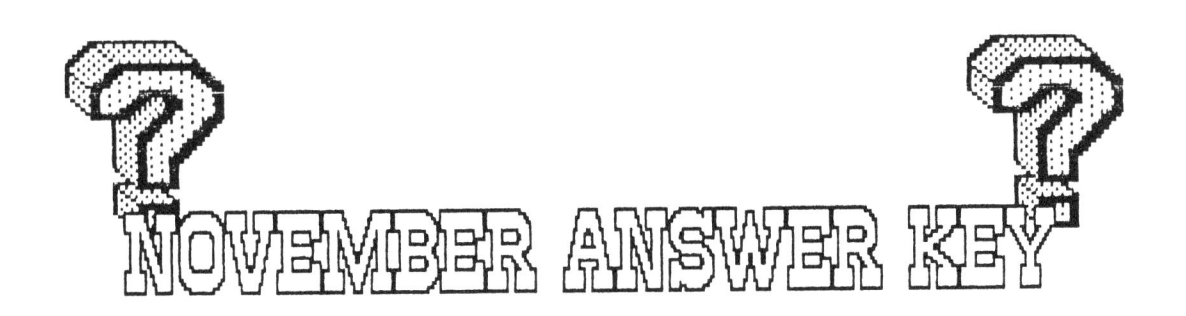

Gail Haley: *A Story, a Story*

1. stories
2. leopard, teeth
3. hornets
4. fairy
5. sticky
6. spun
7. golden
8. Africa
9. smart

Nathaniel Benchley: *The Strange Disappearance of Arthur Cluck*

1. chicken
2. head
3. gone
4. duck
5. rooster
6. owl
7. fox
8. colored
9. truck
10. ride

Ed Young: *Lon Po Po*

1. 3; 1
2. don't let anyone in; don't talk to strangers
3. mother; Little Red Riding Hood
4. grandmother; grandmother
5. wolf killed by children; depends on version

NOVEMBER AUTHORS BIBLIOGRAPHY

November 4   Gail Haley
A Story, A Story (Macmillan, 1970)—1971 Caldecott Award; *Birdsong* (Crown, 1984); *Jack and the Bean Tree* (Crown, 1986); *Jack and the Fire Dragon* (Crown, 1988)

November 9   Lois Ehlert
All published by HBJ: *Growing Vegetable Soup* (1987); *Planting a Rainbow* (1988); *Color Zoo* (1989)—1990 Caldecott Honor Book; *Eating the Alphabet* (1989); *Feathers for Lunch* (1990); *Fish Eyes: A Book You Can Count On* (1990); illustrator for *Chicka Chicka Boom Boom* by Martin & Archambault (Simon & Schuster, 1989)

November 13   Nathaniel Benchley
Red Fox and His Canoe (Harper, 1964); *Oscar Otter* (Harper, 1966); *The Strange Disappearance of Arthur Cluck* (Harper, 1967); *Sam the Minuteman* (Harper, 1969); *Several Tricks of Edgar Dolphin* (Harper, 1970); *Small Wolf* (Harper, 1972); *A Ghost Named Fred* (Harper, 1979); *Walter the Homing Pigeon* (Harper, 1981); *George the Drummer Boy* (Harper, 1987)

November 14   Alan Baker
Benjamin's Portrait (Lothrop, 1987)

November 16   Victoria Chess
Illustrator for *Once Around the Block* by Kevin Henkes (see November 27)

November 16   Jean Fritz
These lively historical fiction books are all published by Putnam: *And Then What Happened, Paul Revere?* (1973); *Where Was Patrick Henry on the 29th of May?* (1975); *Who's That Stepping on Plymouth Rock?* (1975); *Will You Sign Here, John Hancock?* (1976); *Where Do You Think You're Going, Christopher Columbus?* (1980); *Can't You Make Them Behave, King George?* (1982); *What's the Big Idea, Ben Franklin?* (1982); *Why Don't You Get a Horse, Sam Adams?* (1982); *Shh! We're Writing the Constitution* (1987)

November 19   Margaret Musgrove
Ashanti to Zulu: African Traditions (Dial, 1976)—1977 Caldecott Award Book

November 19   Ann H. Scott
Sam (McGraw-Hill, 1967); *On Mother's Lap* (McGraw-Hill, 1972); *Someday Rider* (Houghton, 1989)

November 20   William Cole
Beastly Boys and Ghastly Girls (Dell, 1977); *Oh, Such Foolishness* (Harper, 1978); *Poem Stew* (Harper, 1981); *Monster Knock Knocks* (Simon & Schuster, 1988); *Oh, That's Ridiculous* (Penguin, 1988)

November Authors Bibliography

November 27   Kevin Henkes

All published by Greenwillow: *Clean Enough* (1982); *Grandpa and Bo* (1982); *Margaret and Taylor* (1983); *Return to Sender* (1984); *Bailey Goes Camping* (1985); *Weekend with Wendell* (1986); *Once Around the Block* (1987); *Sheila Rae the Brave* (1987); *Chester's Way* (1988); *Jessica* (1989); *Zebra Wall* (1989)

November 28   Ed Young

Lon Po Po (Philomel, 1989)—1990 Caldecott Award Book; illustrator for: *The Girl Who Loved the Wind* by Jane Yolen (Crowell, 1972); *The Lion and the Mouse* (Doubleday, 1979); *White Wave: A Chinese Tale* (Crowell, 1979); *Yeh-Shen: A Cinderella Story from Japan* (Philomel, 1982); *The Other Bone* (Harper, 1984); *I Wish I Were a Butterfly* by James Howe (HBJ, 1987); *Birches* by Robert Frost (Holt, 1988); *Cats Are Cats* (Philomel, 1988)

November 28   Stephanie Calmenson

The Birthday Hat (Putnam, 1983); *Ten Furry Monsters* (Parents, 1984); *The Giggle Book* (Parents, 1987); *One Little Monkey* (Crown, 1987); *The Principal's New Clothes* (Scholastic, 1989); *What Am I? Very First Riddles* (Harper, 1989)

DECEMBER

December 1	Jan Brett, *Beauty and the Beast* (investigating details)
December 2	David Macaulay, *Black and White* (reading appreciation)
December 3	Hugh Lewin, *Jafta's Father* (writing activity)*
December 5	Phyllis Adams, *Hi, Dog!* (writing activity)
December 7	Ellen Weiss, *Millicent Maybe* (fill in)
December 9	Adelaide Holl, *Rain Puddle* (fill in/writing activity)
December 10	Barbara Gregorich, *Nine Men Chase a Hen* (fill in)
December 16	Ruth Stiles Gannett, *My Father's Dragon* (making predictions)
December 22	Jerry Pinkney, *Pretend You're a Cat* (writing/drawing activity)*
December 27	Ted Rand, *Country Crossing* (descriptive writing *activity*)
December 29	Molly Bang, *Ten, Nine, Eight* (writing activity)*

December Bookmarks
December Answer Key
December Authors Bibliography

*Denotes multicultural title/activity

DECEMBER AUTHORS

DATE	NAME	AUTHOR	ILLUSTRATOR	K	1	2	3
1	Jan Brett	X	X	X	X	X	
2	David Macaulay	X	X	X	X	X	X
3	Hugh Lewin	X					
5	Phyllis Adams	X		X	X	X	
5	Harve Zemach	X	X			X	X
7	Ellen Weiss	X		X	X		
9	Jean de Brunhoff	X	X	X	X	X	
9	Adelaide Holl	X		X	X	X	X
10	Barbara Gregorich	X		X	X		
12	Barbara Emberley	X				X	X
14	Lorna Balian	X	X	X	X	X	
16	Ruth Stiles Gannett	X					X
16	Marie Hall Ets	X		X	X	X	X
16	Quentin Blake	X	X			X	X
19	Eve Bunting	X				X	X
21	Michael Berenstain	X		X	X	X	
22	Jerry Pinkney		X	X	X	X	X
25	Eth Clifford	X					X
26	Jean Van Leeuwen	X			X	X	
27	Ted Rand		X	X	X	X	
29	Molly Bang	X					
30	Mercer Mayer	X	X	X	X	X	X

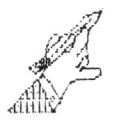

JAN BRETT

Beauty and the Beast

Read *Beauty and the Beast*. Jan read many versions before she wrote her own. There are special messages and pictures in her illustrations. If you look very carefully, you will see what Beauty cannot.

A fairy spell has changed all the members of the Beast's household into animals. Look at page 5 for the first clue. A monkey carries a tray of fruit. Is he really a monkey?

Jan has also placed sayings above certain tapestries (wall coverings woven like rugs). The first is: "Be guided by your heart's gratitude."

Find these sayings. Write what they mean in the story.

1. Be guided by your heart's gratitude.
   _____
   _____

2. Do not_____
   _____
   _____

3. Your happiness_____
   _____
   _____

4. Courage, Beauty _____
   _____
   _____

Name _____ Date _____

DAVID MACAULAY
Black and White

NOTE TO THE TEACHER: *Black and White* by David Macaulay is a very special kind of Caldecott Award book. The 1991 winner has opened new territory for young as well as older readers. This book requires a very special type of presentation. You may find this suggestion helpful.

1. Tell the children you have a very different kind of story to share with them.

2. Show them the first double page spread and read the titles. Tell them to choose a story to follow as you turn the pages. Tell them they will read the pictures instead of listening to the story.

3. Arrange them in four groups so that children interested in the same story can share visual perceptions as you turn the pages.

4. When you are finished turning the pages, start again at the beginning and ask the children which pictures they liked best. Ask them how the stories are related. Ask them if each individual story would have been a good book or not. Ask them to explain and support their answers.

5. Read each story individually, asking children to notice how the other stories relate to the one being read.

6. Leave the book on a table or counter for a week or two for reading or viewing pleasure.

HUGH LEWIN

Jafta's Father

Read *Jafta's Father*. Jafta's father works in the city. This story is a collection of memories and longing for him to return in the spring.

Your father does things for you, too, I'm sure. Use the lines below to write a rough draft of a story about the favorite things your father does for you. If you do not live with your father, you can write about another person who does wonderful things with you.

_____

_____

_____

_____

_____

_____

_____

Name _____   Date _____

PHYLLIS ADAMS

Hi, Dog!

Read *Hi, Dog!* Use the words from the Word Bank to remember what presents the Troll family received.

1. Leona wanted a dog, but she got _____.

2. Wendall wanted a dog, but he got _____.

3. Blossom wanted a dog, but she got a big _____.

4. Buddy wanted a dog, but he got a big pile of _____.

5. Etta wanted a dog, but she got _____.

6. Then, the _____ came to the house.

7. The Troll family was finally _____.

8. They named the dog _____.

Word Bank

| balloons | cake | dog | Dandy | happy |
| hats | ice cream | party | presents | |

Name _____   Date _____

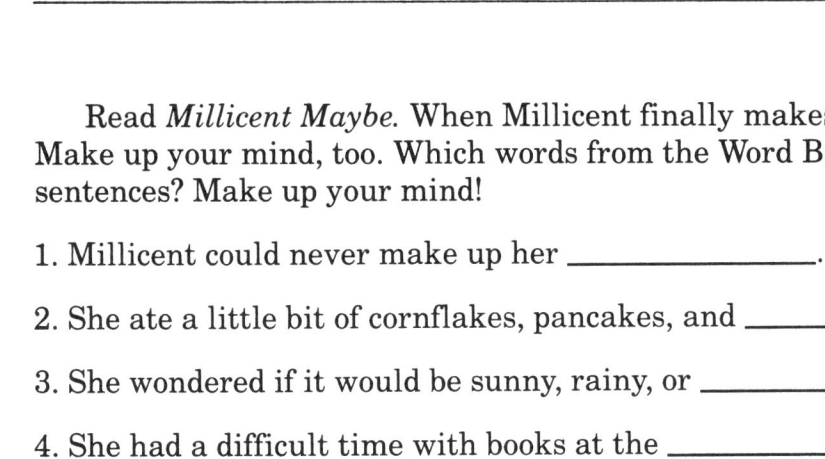

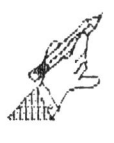

ELLEN WEISS

Millicent Maybe

Read *Millicent Maybe*. When Millicent finally makes up her mind, she's happy. Make up your mind, too. Which words from the Word Bank go in the spaces in the sentences? Make up your mind!

1. Millicent could never make up her _____.

2. She ate a little bit of cornflakes, pancakes, and _____.

3. She wondered if it would be sunny, rainy, or _____.

4. She had a difficult time with books at the _____.

5. She never knew which _____ to buy at the shoe store.

6. One day, her _____ didn't fit.

7. She went to the pet store and bought a few _____.

8. One screamed, "Take a _____."

9. Another cried, "Make _____."

10. Finally, Millicent set the parrots _____.

11. She decided to keep what she liked _____.

Word Bank					
bath	best	clothes	cold	free	library
mind	parrots	popcorn	shoes	toast	

Name _____ Date _____

ADELAIDE HOLL

Rain Puddle

Read *Rain Puddle*. Adelaide Holl wrote the story and Roger Duvoisin drew the pictures about several silly barnyard animals. Use the words in the Word Bank to fill in the blanks in the sentences.

1. Plump hen was _____ in the grass.

2. Turkey was eating _____.

3. Pig was crunching _____.

4. Sheep was _____ clover in the _____.

5. Cow was _____ her _____ in the shade.

6. In the end, wise old owl just _____.

Word Bank

| apples | chewing | chuckled | corn |
| cud | meadow | nibbling | pecking |

Adelaide didn't tell us what these other farm animals were doing. Finish the sentences below. Add a verb and a place as Adelaide did in the story.

7. Cat was _____ in the _____.

8. Dog was _____ by the _____.

9. Donkey was _____ near her _____.

10. Rooster was _____ on the _____.

11. Little mouse was _____ next to the _____.

Name _____ Date _____

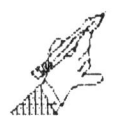

BARBARA GREGORICH

Nine Men Chase a Hen

Read *Nine Men Chase a Hen*. Use the words from the Word Bank to fill in the blanks of this story reminder.

1. This is a story of _____ and _____.

2. Hens like to wear _____.

3. But that makes a man _____.

4. The men have a pet _____.

5. The pet _____ the hens.

6. Then, they _____ about how they _____.

7. The hens turn on many _____.

8. Angry hens _____ the men.

9. The men are _____. They bring _____.

10. The men and hens become _____.

Word Bank

chase	corn	elephant	fight	friends	hats	hens
laugh	lights	men	sorry	splashes	write	

Name _____   Date _____

RUTH STILES GANNETT

My Father's Dragon

Good readers are always listening to themselves read. They hear the story as well as see it with their eyes. A good reader also makes predictions. If you are really into a story, you will try to guess what's going to happen next. Read Chapter I of *My Father's Dragon*. Write several events that you think will happen next.

Think of predictions for Chapter 2. Write your predictions below. Read Chapter 2 to see if you are right.

Make predictions whenever you feel you know what is going to happen. A prediction sheet follows this one. Have fun making predictions. They will make you a better reader!

    Elmer and the cat will go to Wild Island.

    They will meet nice animals on the island and have an adventure.

    The island was messy so the cat was sad.

_____

_____

_____

_____

Name _____ Date _____

Prediction Sheet

_____

_____

_____

_____

_____

_____

_____

Name _____ **Date** _____

JERRY PINKNEY

Pretend You're a Cat

Read *Pretend You're a Cat*. Jean wrote the book, but only Jerry Pinkney could make it come so alive with his pictures. This book makes me feel like writing. How about you?

Write your own *Pretend You're a* _____ book. Your pictures may not be as wonderful as Jerry's, but draw pictures to go with your story. What will you be? Use the lines below to write ideas that you will need for your story.

_____
_____
_____
_____
_____
_____
_____
_____
_____
_____
_____
_____
_____
_____
_____
_____

Name _____ Date _____

TED RAND
Country Crossing

Read *Country Crossing*. Ted's pictures are so beautiful. He did a wonderful job of SHOWING us how the moon can light up the country at night.

Jim Aylesworth did a great job of TELLING us how the sounds of a train, the moonlight, the sounds of insects and animals all combine to make a special time for a little boy.

Select an event and write a story about it. You can write about the sights, sounds, and feelings of going to bed, a trip to Grandma's, Christmas Eve, or whatever you want. Draw your own pictures to go with your story. Use the lines below to write ideas for the rough draft of your story.

_____

_____

_____

_____

_____

_____

_____

_____

Name _____   Date _____

MOLLY BANG

Ten, Nine, Eight

Read *Ten, Nine, Eight*. Molly has written and drawn a very lovely good-night story. We can do one, too, or write a wake-up story that starts with 1 and ends with 10.

Here is a wake-up example:

One little hungry boy waking up late,
Dreams of two eggs and three sausages on a plate.

Four knocks on the door
tell him he has five minutes
to get his feet on the floor.

Six toothbrushes by the sink—his is pink.

Seven pairs of jeans. He wants thirteen.

Eight shirts, but only one is clean.

Nine shoes, but none is a pair.

Down the stairs, ten seconds to spare.

"You're late. We already ate."
"You can do the dishes! HA HA!"

Name _____ Date _____

December Primary I

☆ Jan Brett
☆ Harve Zemach
☆ Jean de Brunhoff
☆ Lorna Balian
☆ Marie Hall Ets
☆ Michael Berenstain
☆ Hugh Lewin
☆ Phyllis Adams

December
Primary I

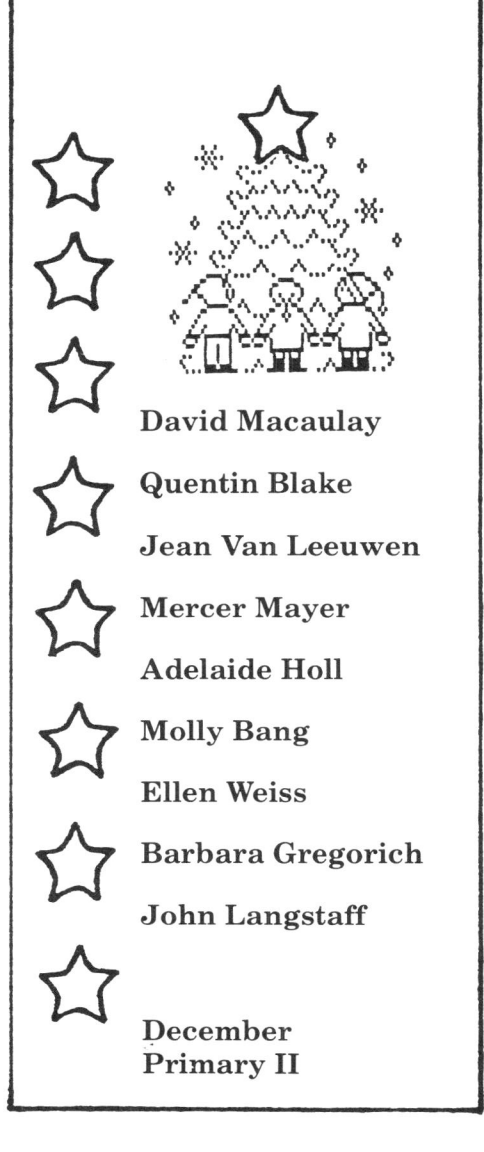

December Primary II

☆ David Macaulay
☆ Quentin Blake
☆ Jean Van Leeuwen
☆ Mercer Mayer
☆ Adelaide Holl
☆ Molly Bang
☆ Ellen Weiss
☆ Barbara Gregorich
☆ John Langstaff

December
Primary II

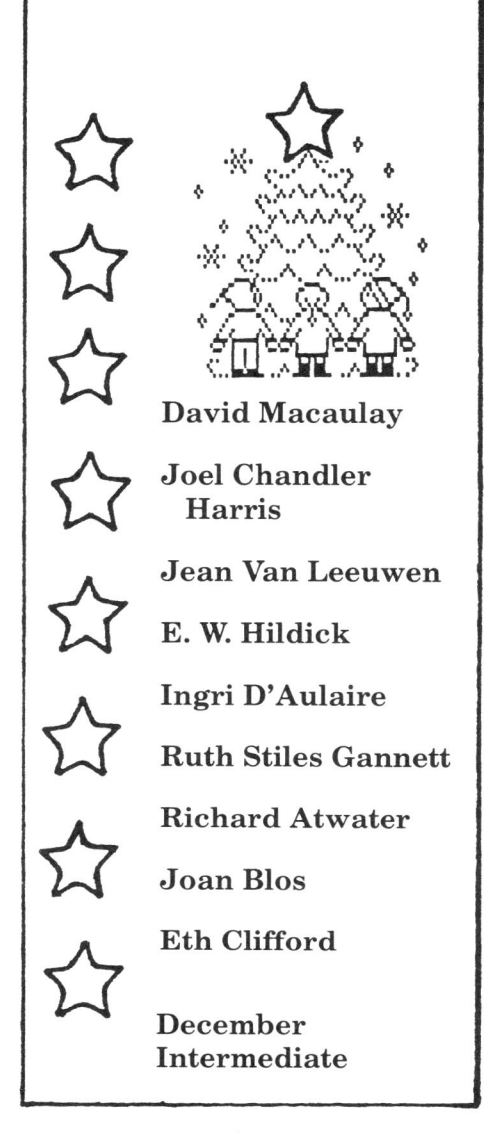

December Intermediate

☆ David Macaulay
☆ Joel Chandler Harris
☆ Jean Van Leeuwen
☆ E. W. Hildick
☆ Ingri D'Aulaire
☆ Ruth Stiles Gannett
☆ Richard Atwater
☆ Joan Blos
☆ Eth Clifford

December
Intermediate

DECEMBER ANSWER KEY

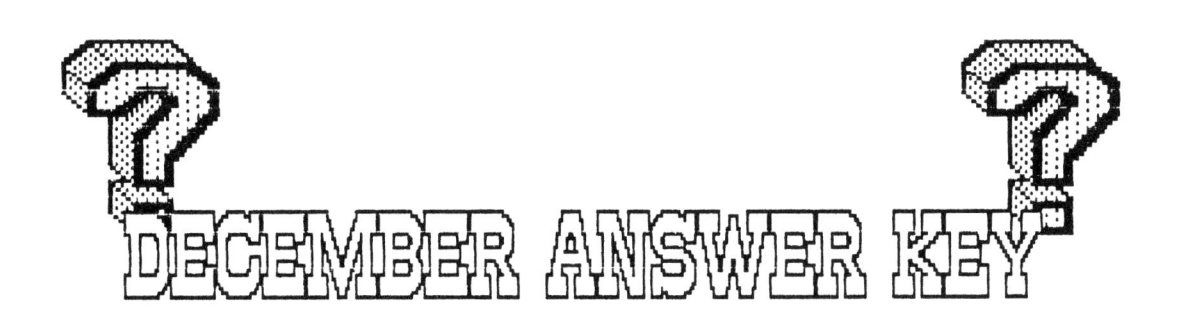

Jan Brett: *Beauty and the Beast*

Answers will vary. Examples are:

1. "Be guided by your heart's gratitude." Do what you believe is right when your heart is happy.

2. "Do not trust to appearance:" Do not judge a book by its cover. Look at what a person does—not how he or she looks.

3. "Your happiness is not far away:" In the story, Beauty will soon be happy. Or the Beast, her future happiness, is near.

4. "Courage, Beauty:" Trust the kindness of the Beast. You are loved and safe.

Phyllis Adams, *Hi, Dog!*
1. balloons
2. ice cream
3. cake
4. presents
5. party hats
6. dog
7. happy
8. Dandy

Ellen Weiss: *Millicent Maybe*
1. mind
2. toast
3. cold
4. library
5. shoes
6. clothes
7. parrots
8. bath
9. popcorn
10. free
11. best

Adelaide Holl: *Rain Puddle*
1. pecking
2. corn
3. apples
4. nibbling; meadow
5. chewing; cud
6. chuckled
7-11. Answers will vary

Barbara Gregorich: *Nine Men Chase a Hen*
1. men; hens
2. hats
3. laugh
4. elephant
5. splashes
6. fight; write
7. lights
8. chase
9. sorry; corn
10. friends

DECEMBER AUTHORS BIBLIOGRAPHY

December 1 Jan Brett

Fritz and the Beautiful Horses (Houghton, 1981); *Annie and the Wild Animals* (Houghton, 1985); *The Twelve Days of Christmas* (Putnam, 1986); *Goldilocks and the Three Bears* (Putnam, 1987); *The First Dog* (HBJ, 1988); *Beauty and the Beast* (Clarion, 1989); *The Mitten* (Putnam, 1989): *The Owl and the Pussycat* (Putnam, 1991)

December 2 David Macaulay

All published by Houghton-Mifflin: *Cathedral* (1973)—1974 Caldecott Honor Book; *Pyramid* (1975); *Underground* (1976); *Castle* (1977)—1978 Caldecott Honor Book; *BAAA* (1985); *City: A Story of Roman Planning and Construction* (1983); *Unbuilding* (1987); *Why the Chicken Crossed the Road* (1987); *How Things Work* (1988); *Mill* (1989); *Black and White* (1990)—1991 Caldecott Award Book

December 3 Hugh Lewin

All published by Carolrhoda: *Jafta* (1983); *Jafta and the Wedding* (1983); *Jafta's Mother* (1983); *Jafta: The Journey* (1984); *Jafta: The Town* (1984); *Jafta's Father* (1989)

December 5 Phyllis Adams

Easy-to-read series, each published by Modern Curriculum Press: Pippin series—*Pippin at the Gym; Pippin Cleans Up; Pippin Eats Out; Pippin Goes to Work;* Troll Family series—*A Dog Is Not a Troll; Go, Wendall, Go; Hi, Dog!; A Troll, a Truck, and a Cookie; Good Show; I Love Wheels*

December 7 Ellen Weiss

Bean series published by Troll Associates: *Starring Green Bean; Half-Baked Bean; Bean Sprout; Boston Bean; Jelly Bean; Lima Bean; Mean Bean; Vanilla Bean*

December 9 Adelaide Holl

Rain Puddle (Lothrop, 1965); *Remarkable Egg* (Lothrop, 1968); Small Bear series published by Garrard: *Bedtime for Bears; Small Bear and the Secret Surprise; Small Bear Builds a Playhouse; Small Bear Solves a Mystery; Small Bear's Birthday Party; Small Bear's Busy Day; Small Bear's Name Hunt; Wake Up, Small Bear*

December 10 Barbara Gregorich

Dirty Proof (Crown, 1988); all published by School Zone Publishing, 1984-1985: *Nine Men Chase a Hen; Fox on the Box; Beep-Beep; Elephant and Envelope; Gum on the Drum; I Want a Pet; It's Magic; Jace, Mace and the Big Race; Jog, Frog, Jog; My Friend Goes Left; Say Good Night; Sue Likes Blue*

December 16 Ruth Stiles Gannett

My Father's Dragon (Random, 1948); *The Dragons of Blueland* (Random, 1963); *Elmer and the Dragon* (Random, 1964)

December 22 Jerry Pinkney

Illustrator of: *The Patchwork Quilt* by Valerie Flournoy (Dial, 1985); *Tales of Brer Rabbit* by Julius Lester (Dial, 1987); *Mirandy and Brother Wind* by Patricia McKissack (Knopf, 1988)—1989 Caldecott Honor Book; *More Tales of Brer Rabbit* by Julius Lester (Dial, 1988); *Rabbit Makes a Monkey of Lion* by Verna Aardema (Dial, 1989); *Turtle in July* by Marilyn Singer (Macmillan, 1989); *Pretend You're a Cat* by Jean Marzollo (Dial, 1990)

December 27 Ted Rand

Illustrator of: *The Ghost-Eye Tree* by Bill Martin and John Archamabult (Holt, 1985); *Barn Dance* by Bill Martin and John Archamabult (Holt, 1986); *White Dynamite and Curly Kidd* by Bill Martin and John Archamabult (Holt, 1986) *Knots on a Counting Rope* by Bill Martin and John Archamabult (Holt, 1987); *Country Crossing* by Jim Aylesworth (Holt, 1990)

December 29 Molly Bang

The Grey Lady and the Strawberry Snatcher (Macmillan, 1980); *Dawn* (Morrow, 1983); *Ten, Nine, Eight* (Penguin, 1985); *Wiley and the Hairy Man* (Macmillan, 1987)

JANUARY

January 1	Barbara Williams, *Kevin's Grandma* (writing activity)
January 4	Fernando Krahn, *Mystery of the Giant Footprints* (writing activity)
January 7	Kay Chorao, *George Told Kate* (word meanings)
January 9	Clyde Robert Bulla, *Dandelion Hill* (fill in)
January 11	Ann Tompert, *Grandfather Tang's Story* (tangrams)*
January 22	Margaret Hillert, *Dear Dragon* (say and search)
January 22	Brian Wildsmith, *The Lazy Bear* (fill in)
January 28	Ann Jonas, *Reflections, Round Trip, The Trek* (letter writing)
January 28	Vera B. Williams, *"More, More, More," Said the Baby** (writing activity)
January 30	Tony Johnston, *Happy Birthday, Mole and Troll* (wordsearch)

January Bookmarks
January Answer Key
January Authors Bibliography

*Denotes multicultural title/activity

JANUARY AUTHORS

DATE	NAME	AUTHOR/ILLUSTRATOR		K	1	2	3
1	Barbara Williams	X		X	X	X	
3	Joan Walsh Anglund	X	X	X	X	X	
3	Carolyn Haywood	X			X	X	
4	Jacob Grimm	X				X	X
4	Fernando Krahn	X	X	X	X	X	X
6	Carl Sandburg	X				X	X
7	Kay Chorao	X	X	X	X	X	
9	Clyde Robert Bulla	X					X
11	Ann Tompert	X		X	X	X	X
18	Raymond Briggs	X	X	X	X	X	
18	A. A. Milne	X		X	X	X	X
22	Margaret Hillert	X		X	X		
22	Blair Lent	X		X	X	X	X
22	Brian Wildsmith	X	X		X		
27	Lewis Carroll	X					X
27	Harry Allard	X		X	X	X	
28	Ann Jonas	X	X	X	X	X	
28	Vera B. Williams	X	X	X	X	X	
29	Bill Peet	X	X			X	X
29	Rosemary Wells	X	X		X	X	
30	Lloyd Alexander	X					X
30	Tony Johnston	X		X	X	X	
31	Gerald McDermott	X	X			X	X

BARBARA WILLIAMS

Kevin's Grandma

Read *Kevin's Grandma*. Barbara and Kay, the illustrator, were both born in January—Barbara on the 1st and Kay on the 7th.

What is your grandmother like? To answer these questions about your grandmother, you will need to interview her. Then write a little story about her.

My grandmother loves to _____.

_____

Life would be boring if Grandma didn't _____.

She's the only one in the family who can

_____

I'll never forget the time Grandmother _____

_____

My grandmother likes to laugh about _____

_____

_____ makes my grandmother sad.

My favorite time with Grandma was _____

_____

_____.

Name _____ Date _____

FERNANDO KRAHN

Mystery of the Giant Footprints

Look at the pictures in *April Fools, Little Love Story, Mystery of the Giant Footprints, Amanda and the Mysterious Carpet, The Creepy Thing, Secret in the Dungeon,* or any other book by Fernando Krahn. He is an expert at telling stories with only pictures.

Try to write the story that goes with one of Krahn's books. Type your story on 3″ X 5″ self-stick notes. When the story is done, place the notes on the correct page. Now the story is written by you and illustrated by Fernando Krahn. Aren't you lucky to work with a great illustrator? You'll be famous! Share your story with your classmates.

Name _____   **Date** _____

KAY CHORAO

George Told Kate

Read *George Told Kate*. Use the words from the Word Bank to match the words with their meanings.

1. _ _ _ _ _ _   place to learn
2. _ _ _ _ _   with paper and pencil
3. _ _ _ _   do this to books
4. _ _ _ _   change where you live
5. _ _ _ _ _   bigger machine than a car
6. _ _ _ _   not the country
7. _ _ _ _ _   fool someone
8. _ _ _ _ _ _   Kate's brother

Word Bank							
city	George	move	read	school	tease	truck	write

On the back of this paper, draw a picture of the thing your brother and sister teases you about the most.

Name _____ Date _____

CLYDE ROBERT BULLA

Dandelion Hill

Read *Dandelion Hill*. Use the words in the Word Bank to finish these sentences about Violet at Red Barn Farm.

1. _____ was the new cow at Red Barn Farm.

2. The cows asked her to come along and eat _____.

3. She went to _____ Hill to play.

4. The calves _____ down the hill and across the bridge.

5. Violet broke the _____.

6. The next day they had a _____.

7. Violet ate the _____ in one bite.

8. Violet jumped too high and landed in a _____.

9. The next day, Violet _____ with the cows.

10. At night, Violet _____ with the moon on Dandelion Hill.

Word Bank				
bridge	cake	danced	Dandelion	grass
grazed	picnic	skipped	tree	Violet

Name _____ Date _____

ANN TOMPERT

Grandfather Tang's Story

NOTE TO TEACHER: Read *Grandfather Tang's Story*. But before you do, select one of these activities to do with the children.

1. Photocopy and cut out the tangrams on the back page. Place them on an overhead projector, and practice putting them together to form the shapes of the animals as you tell the story. They lay better on the overhead projector if they are glued to lightweight tagboard. The paper alone has a tendency to curl.

2. Tell the story a second time. Ask children to arrange the tangram correctly on the overhead. Remind them that tans may only touch, not overlap. You must use all the pieces.

3. Photocopy the tangrams at the end of the book for each child. Have the children cut them out and arrange into the shapes you have on the overhead. For this section you could make a transparency of the animal tans from the story as a guide for students to follow.

4. Use a large piece of black construction paper to make oversize tangrams. Have children work on a table to make the shapes of animals in the story.

5. At the end of the story, Wu Ling changes into a lion and chases the hunter away. What other animal could he have changed into? Can you arrange your tangrams in that shape?

6. Have children try to create their own animal shapes and write a story to go with them. Or they can build any kind of shape from the tans to go with a story.

MARGARET HILLERT

Dear Dragon

In the wordsearch puzzle, you will find words from the *Dear Dragon* books by Margaret Hillert. Say all the words to a friend. Then find the words in the puzzle. When you finish the puzzle, read all the *Dear Dragon* books you can find.

```
K A O S S E P R D K H O C A N G M
K R E T B B I G N E B F X W Z C S
K U D X B I P Q R R L I R A C T H
B F Q F O R G B U F U N N Y A L L
B F K E A T F D R A E D E A R O B
V O W D C H R I S T M A S W X S L
P J W I S D I D W H A R H G T H P
H W F G C A E R G E T E X G N I Y
D D L H D Y N D B R D A Y Q J J C
J D D Z C B D R A G O N U K C U B
C O O K I E S E L T W O Q G U I P
G A X C Y A N A L A N D V C Q H E
H J A M V S Y M S M B N A S U P V
M B A B Y T W D A T H P P B N A U
N U C O M E K S O Y L H F F W Y Y
H T G O Y R F O W S U Q P Q I W K
M E R K M K U A K D H J T X C E P
```

CHRISTMAS	BIRTHDAY	FRIENDS
COOKIES	FATHER	EASTER
DRAGON	FUNNY	DREAM
BALLS	FIND	DOWN
DEAR	COME	BOOK
BLUE	BABY	AWAY
GET	FUN	FOR
EAT	DID	DAY
CAR	CAN	BUT
BIG	ARE	AND
ALL	GO	DO
BE	AT	AM
A		

Name _____   Date _____

BRIAN WILDSMITH

The Lazy Bear

Read *The Lazy Bear*. Use the words in the Word Bank to finish these sentences about a nice, but lazy bear.

1. _____ was usually nice to his friends.

2. One day, he found a _____.

3. It _____ down the hill. He liked that.

4. He didn't like _____ it up the hill.

5. He found his friends: goat, deer and _____.

6. They enjoyed the _____.

7. They didn't like pushing the wagon up the _____.

8. _____ had an idea.

9. Bear ended up in a _____. The animals _____ at him.

10. Bear learned to share the _____.

Word Bank

bear	goat	hill	laughed	pond
pushing	raccoon	ride	rolled	wagon	work

Name _____ Date _____

ANN JONAS

Reflections; Round Trip; The Trek

Read *Reflections, Round Trip,* or *The Trek*. Ann Jones has created a story that is twice as long as most other stories. Read from the beginning to the end, turn it over, and read from the back to the front.

She works very hard at her craft. Select two pictures from the story. Write several sentences about each picture explaining why you like them. Send Ann a note telling her what a wonderful artist she is.

If you enjoy the work of Donald Crews, you can tell her too. They are married. Include a note about Donald's work if you have read *Freight Train, Carousel, Flying, Harbor, Truck,* or *School Bus*.

Ann Jonas
c/o Greenwillow Books
103 Madison Avenue
New York, NY 10016

Picture 1 _____

_____

_____

_____

_____

_____

Picture 2 _____

_____

_____

_____

_____

_____

Name _____ Date _____

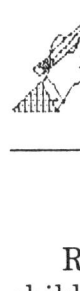

VERA B. WILLIAMS

"More, More, More," Said the Baby

Read *"More, More, More," Said the Baby*. Vera wrote this story for her grandchildren. The subtitle for this book is *3 Love Stories*. You can tell after reading this book that daddies, grandmas, and mommies love their children. But there are many people who love children. Pick three of them and write a short love story about how different people love children.

Below is a list of people to consider. Or pick your own.
Use the lines below to write your rough draft ideas.

People who love children:

aunts, uncles, cousins, grandpas, neighbors, teachers, police officers, firefighters, doctors, principals, crossing guards, bus drivers

_____

_____

_____

_____

_____

_____

Name _____ Date _____

TONY JOHNSTON
Happy Birthday, Mole and Troll

Read *Happy Birthday, Mole and Troll*. There are four stories and each one is funnier than the one before it. Find the words in the wordsearch puzzle below.

```
T C N I K Q Z O Z U G Z H U O P P
F J A J K D I S S O R M M W J D L
W J C N J N T D I M O O C I L I P
M X U C D N A P D O O V W S K V L
K R Y I A L L I B R E A T H X O I
T Q H V P K E W H O A A Z J Z W E
C L W X P R E S E N T G J L G U S
H Z M J V K U U U P S T O N E P P
A O J Y A M I R R O R Y K N I A L
A S I K Z X L P X C C R E K Z S F
J H P W U V B R O F L A S H H A O
J Z D D L I F I R E L I R N V R Q
A E F B J M X S R U M N Z D C H S
W R D T W Y K E L T W H K D I O K
Y E P V S O E O X X H U W M Y J U
E C P G A N F R V I B D Z X R B O
U D O P C F C C M U M H A Y Y S I
W D C P I W P B Q S L K U Y U Q O
```

BIRTHDAY   SURPRISE   MUSHROOM
PRESENT   CANDLES   MIRROR
DRAGON   BREATH   JOKES
TRUNK   FLASH   STONE
CAKE   CARD   POEM
RAIN   BOOM   FIRE
WISH   LEAF   ANTS
SKIP

Name _____   Date _____

Raymond Briggs

Crosby Bonsall
Carolyn Haywood
Margaret Hillert
Ann Jonas
Fernando Krahn
Ann Tompert
Vera B. Williams
Joan Walsh Anglund

January
Primary I

Harry Allard

Kay Chorao
Jacob Grimm
A. A. Milne
Rosemary Wells
Barbara Williams
Brian Wildsmith
Tony Johnston

January
Primary II

Bill Peet

Lee J. Ames
Clyde Robert Bulla
Lewis Carroll
Carl Sandburg
Michael Bond
Hugh Lofting
A. A. Milne

January
Intermediate

JANUARY ANSWER KEY

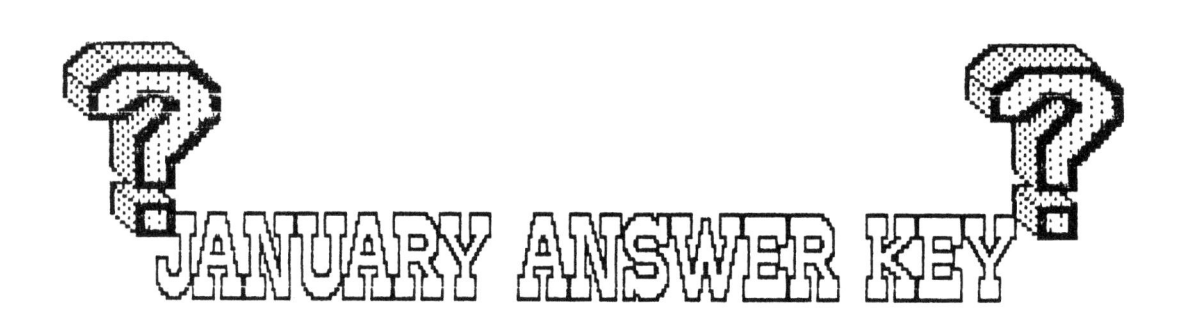

Kay Chorao: *George Told Kate*

1. school
2. write
3. read
4. move
5. truck
6. city
7. tease
8. George

Clyde Robert Bulla: *Dandelion Hill*

1. Violet
2. grass
3. Dandelion
4. skipped
5. bridge
6. picnic
7. cake
8. tree
9. grazed
10. danced

Margaret Hillert: *Dear Dragon*

Some solutions will vary.

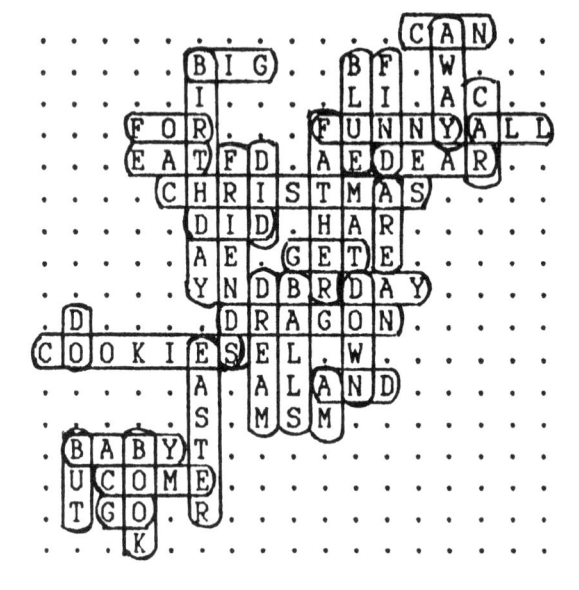

January Answer Key

Brian Wildsmith: *The Lazy Bear*

1. bear
2. wagon
3. rolled
4. pushing
5. raccoon
6. ride
7. hill
8. goat
9. pond, laughed
10. work

Tony Johnston: *Happy Birthday, Mole and Troll*

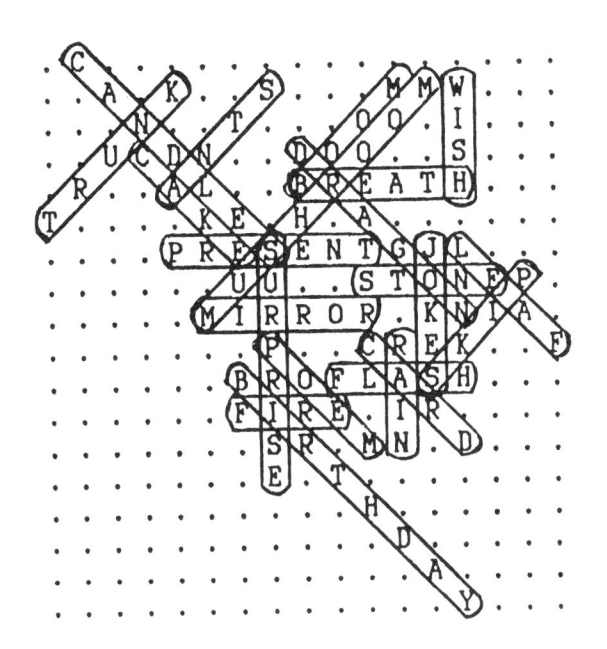

JANUARY AUTHORS BIBLIOGRAPHY

January 1 Barbara Williams

Albert's Toothache, illustrated by Kay Chorao (Dutton, 1974); *Kevin's Grandma* (Dutton, 1975); *Chester Chipmunk's Thanksgiving* (Dutton, 1978); *Jeremy Isn't Hungry* (Dutton, 1978); *Horrible, Impossible, Bad Witch Child* (Avon, 1982); *Mitzi and the Terrible Tyrannosaurus Rex* (Dutton, 1982); *Mitzi and Frederick the Great* (Dutton, 1984); *Mitzi and the Elephants* (Dutton, 1985)

January 4 Fernando Krahn

Illustrator of the following very funny wordless picture books: *April Fools* (Dutton, 1974); *Little Love Story* (Lippincott, 1976); *Mystery of the Giant's Footprints* (Dutton, 1977); *The Creepy Thing* (Houghton Mifflin, 1982); *Secret in the Dungeon* (Houghton Mifflin, 1983); *Amanda and the Mysterious Carpet* (Houghton Mifflin, 1985)

January 7 Kay Chorao

Kay has illustrated the best work of others. She has also illustrated her own best stories: *Molly's Moe* (Houghton Mifflin, 1979); *Oink & Pearl* (Harper, 1981); *Car* (Dutton, 1982); *Kate's Box* (Dutton, 1982); *Quilt* (Dutton, 1982); *Snowman* (Dutton, 1982); *Ups & Downs with Oink & Pearl* (Harper, 1986); *George Told Kate* (Dutton, 1987)

January 9 Clyde Robert Bulla

Sword in the Tree (Crowell, 1956); *Lincoln's Birthday* (Harper, 1966); *Ghost of Windy Hill* (Crowell, 1968); *Wish at the Top* (Crowell, 1974); *Keep Running, Allen!* (Harper, 1978); *Daniel's Duck* (Harper, 1979); *My Friend the Monster* (Harper, 1980); *Charlie's House* (Harper, 1983); *Cardboard Crown* (Harper, 1984); *Chalk Box Kid* (Random, 1987)

January 11 Ann Tompert

Little Fox Goes to the End of the World (Crown, 1979); *Nothing Sticks Like a Shadow* (Houghton Mifflin, 1984); *The Silver Whistle* (Macmillan, 1988); *Will You Come Back for Me?* (Whitman, 1988); *Grandfather Tang's Story* (Crown, 1990)

January 22 Margaret Hillert

She has written several easy-reading series at 1.1 to 1.9 reading levels, including the *Dear Dragon* titles. Over 40 titles are available from Follett Library Book Company and Story House Corporation.

January Authors Bibliography

January 22 Brian Wildsmith

All published by Oxford University press: *The Hunter and His Dog* (1979); *Seasons* (1980); *Give a Dog a Bone* (1985); *Goat's Trail* (1986); *Giddy Up* (1987); *If I Were You* (1987); *The Island* (1987); *The Lazy Bear* (1987); *Little Wood Duck* (1987); *The Owl and the Woodpecker* (1987); *Squirrels* (1987); *Toot, Toot* (1987)

January 28 Ann Jonas

All published by Greenwillow Books: *Two Bear Cubs* (1982); *When You Were a Baby* (1982); *Holes and Peeks* (1984); *The Quilt* (1984); *Now We Can Go* (1986); *Reflections* (1987); *The Trek* (1989); *Round Trip* (1990)

January 28 Vera B. Williams

All published by Greenwillow Books: *A Chair for My Mother* (1982); *Something Special for Me* (1983); *Music, Music for Everyone* (1984); *Three Days on a River in a Red Canoe* (1984); *Cherries and Cherry Pits* (1986); *Stringbean's Trip to the Shining Sea* (1988); *"More, More, More," Said the Baby* (1990)— 1991 Caldecott Honor Book

January 30 Tony Johnston

Happy Birthday, Mole and Troll (Putnam, 1979); *Four Scary Stories* (Putnam, 1980); *Odd Jobs and Friends* (Putnam, 1982); *The Vanishing Pumpkin* (Putnam, 1983); *The Witch's Hat* (Putnam, 1984); *The Quilt Story* (Putnam, 1985); *Farmer Mack Measures His Pig* (Harper, 1986); *Five Little Foxes and the Snow* (Harper, 1987); *Yonder* (Dial, 1988); *Mole and Troll Trim the Tree* (Dell, 1989); *Night Noises and Other Mole and Troll Stories* (Dell, 1989); *Grandpa's Song* (Dial, 1991)

FEBRUARY

February 1   Rebecca Caudill, *A Certain Small Shepherd* (fill in)

February 2   Judith Viorst, *Alexander & the Terrible, Horrible, No Good, Very Bad Day* (writing activity)
              Judith Viorst, *The Tenth Good Thing About Barney* (questionnaire)

February 10   Franz Brandenberg, "The Scare" from *Leo and Emily's Big Ideas* (fill in)

February 10   Stephen Gammell, *The Relatives Came* (writing activity)

February 12   David Small, *Imogene's Antlers* (writing activity)

February 20   Mary Blount Christian, *The Pet Day Mystery* (stuffed pet activity)*

February 25   True Kelley, *Mice at Bat* (silly stories)

February 27   Henry Wadsworth Longfellow, *Hiawatha* (fill in)*
              Henry Wadsworth Longfellow, "Jemima" (writing poems)

February 27   Uri Shulevitz, *The Magician* (fill in)*

February 29   David R. Collins, *Grandfather Woo Goes to School* (embarrassing moments)*

February Bookmarks
February Answer Key
February Authors Bibliography

*Denotes multicultural title/activity

FEBRUARY AUTHORS

DATE	NAME	AUTHOR/ILLUSTRATOR	READING LEVEL			
			K	1	2	3
2	Rebecca Caudill	X			X	X
2	Judith Viorst	X		X	X	
3	Joan Lowery Nixon	X			X	X
4	Pat Ross	X			X	X
4	Russell Hoban	X		X	X	
7	Charles Dickens	X				X
7	Laura Ingalls Wilder	X				X
8	Adrienne Adams	X	X		X	X
8	Anne Rockwell	X	X	X	X	
9	Dick Gackenbach	X	X	X	X	X
10	Stephen Gammell		X	X	X	X
10	Franz Brandenberg	X	X	X	X	X
11	Jane Yolen	X		X	X	X	X
12	Judy Blume	X				X
12	David Small	X		X	X	
15	Norman Bridwell	X	X	X	X	X
15	Mike Thaler	X		X	X	X
16	Edward Packard	X			X	X
17	Robert Newton Peck	X				X
19	Louis Slobodkin	X				X
20	Mary Blount Christian	X		X	X	X
24	Wilhelm Grimm	X			X	X
25	True Kelley as Kelly Oechsli	X	X		X	X
27	Florence Parry Heide	X			X	X
27	Uri Shulevitz	X	X	X	X	X	X
27	Henry Wadsworth Longfellow	X			X	X
29	David R. Collins	X		X	X	X

REBECCA CAUDILL

A Certain Small Shepherd

Read *A Certain Small Shepherd*. This unusual Christmas story has a very long beginning, but a most special ending. Use the words in the Word Bank to finish these sentences about Jamie and his family.

1. On the night Jamie was _____, his mother _____.

2. Jamie couldn't _____.

3. Jamie helped his father plow the _____.

4. Jamie's father told him the names of _____.

5. Jamie helped his father mend _____.

6. One day, Jamie's father sent him to _____.

7. On Christmas Eve there would be a _____.

8. Jamie's sister made him a shepherd's _____.

9. They decorated the tree in the _____.

10. A wild _____ cancelled the play.

11. A man and woman came to Jamie's _____.

12. The woman had a _____ and Jamie _____.

Word Bank

baby	birds	born	coat	corn	church	died
fences	houses	play	school	snowstorm	spoke	talk

Name _____   Date _____

JUDITH VIORST

Alexander & the Terrible, Horrible, No Good Very Bad Day

Read *Alexander & the Terrible, Horrible, No Good, Very Bad Day.* Everybody has a bad day once in a while. Write three to six sentences that tell about a part of one of your worst days. Put all the sheets together and you will have a class book: "Our Worst Day Ever." You can include the names of your friends in your class to make it more interesting!

_____
title

_____

_____ _____

_____

_____

_____

_____

_____

Name _____ **Date** _____

JUDITH VIORST

The Tenth Good Thing About Barney

Read *The Tenth Good Thing About Barney*. Write ten things that you love about your pet. If you don't have a pet, write ten things you love about one of your friends.

_____

_____

_____

_____

_____

_____

_____

_____

_____

_____

Name _____ Date _____

FRANZ BRANDENBERG

"The Scare" from <u>Leo and Emily's Big Ideas</u>

Read "The Scare" from *Leo and Emily's Big Ideas*. Use the words in the Word Bank to finish these sentences about Leo and Emily's big adventure.

1. Leo and Emily wanted to _____ somebody.

2. Leo told her to hide behind a _____.

3. He told her to _____ doorbells.

4. He told her to dial _____ numbers.

5. He said they could make _____ faces.

6. They dressed up as a _____.

7. They put on dad's good _____.

8. They put on mom's good _____.

9. Mom was _____.

10. They put on some _____ clothes.

11. Emily and Leo scared their _____.

12. Leo looked in the _____. He was scared!

Word Bank

angry	grandmother	hat	mirror	old	ring	scare
scarecrow	scary	suit	telephone	tree		

Name _____ Date _____

STEPHEN GAMMELL

The Relatives Came

Read *The Relatives Came*. Some relatives are fun, some are boring. The relatives created by Cynthia Rylant and drawn by Caldecott medalist Stephen Gammell are a riot looking for a place to happen! Do you have relatives like these? Think about the last time you had relatives over to your house. Write a story about it. Be sure to add exciting FICTIONAL events. Try to illustrate your story with color pencils as Stephen does. Use the lines below for the rough draft of your idea.

_____
title

_____

_____

_____

_____

_____

_____

_____

Name _____ **Date** _____

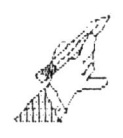

DAVID SMALL

Imogene's Antlers

Read *Imogene's Antlers*. David has quite an imagination. But so do you! If you woke up one morning, what part of your body would be changed? Answer these questions and write a story about the strange thing that happened to your body.

1. How did you change? _____

_____

2. What problems did this cause? _____

_____

_____

3. How was it helpful? _____

_____

_____

4. How did your parents react? What did your friends say?

_____

_____

_____

_____

_____

_____

Name _____ **Date** _____

MARY BLOUNT CHRISTIAN

<u>The Pet Day Mystery</u>

Read *The Pet Day Mystery*. Imagine bringing a pet to school for a day. We can do that, but let's make sure it's stuffed, as in stuffed animals. What is your favorite stuffed animal? Write a 50-word paper explaining why your stuffed animal is your favorite. Display your pet and your paper. If everyone in your room does this activity, you can call it Pet Zoo Day.

My Favorite Stuffed Animal

Name _____ Date _____

TRUE KELLEY/KELLY OECHSLI

Mice at Bat

Read *Mice At Bat*. Imagine mice playing baseball. Fiction books are so much fun when they are silly. Find the silly ideas in this story. There are many. Here are two examples.

Mice do not play baseball.

Mice do not wear clothes.

_____

_____

_____

_____

_____

_____

_____

Name _____ **Date** _____

HENRY WADSWORTH LONGFELLOW

<u>Hiawatha</u>

Read *Hiawatha*, which was written by Longfellow and illustrated by Susan Jeffers. Use the words in the Word Bank to finish these sentences about the brave Indian Hiawatha.

1. By the water stood the _____ of Nokomis.

2. The black and gloomy _____ trees stood near.

3. Nokomis cared for _____.

4. Cry not, for here comes the Naked _____.

5. She taught him about the _____.

6. She showed him the Death-Dance of the _____.

7. He sang to the fireflies "light me with your _____."

8. The rainbow is a heaven for _____.

9. Hooting owls _____ to one another.

10. Hiawatha learned all the names of the _____.

11. He spoke to them in their own _____.

12. He learned all their _____.

13. He called them his _____.

Word Bank

bear	birds	brothers	candle	flowers
Hiawatha	language	pine	secrets	spirits
stars	talk	wigwam		

Name _____ Date _____

HENRY WADSWORTH LONGFELLOW

"Jemima"

Read "Jemima" from *Beastly Boys and Ghastly Girls,* collected by William Cole, World Publishing, 1964.

Other people have added lines to Longfellow's first four lines. Why don't you try it, too? Fill in the lines to get you started. Use rhyming words from the Word Bank below.

One day Jemima went to the zoo

to see what damage she could _____.

She looked around and found a lion,

that wicked girl teased 'im til he started _____.

She found a giraffe and made him laugh,

'til his tired old eyes filled with tears.

Poor thing had a sore throat from his chest to his _____!

Word Bank

cryin   do   ears

WRITE YOUR OWN FOUR LINES OF "JEMIMA" RHYMES BELOW:

_____

_____

_____

_____

Name _____   Date _____

URI SHULEVITZ

The Magician

Read *The Magician*. Use the words in the Word Bank to remember how a magician helps a needy family on the eve of Passover.

1. The magician was _____ and tattered.

2. He was full of _____.

3. He pulled _____ out of his mouth.

4. But he still looked _____.

5. Every table had an extra goblet of _____.

6. Everyone hoped for a special _____.

7. The old man was ready to take his wife to the _____.

8. The magician brought two lighted _____.

9. He brought a cloth for the _____.

10. The _____ moved to the table.

11. Everything they needed _____ out of air.

12. Real food cannot be _____. _____ was their guest.

Word Bank

appears	benches	candlesticks	Elijah	evil	guest
neighbors	poor	ragged ribbons	table	tricks	wine

Name _____   Date _____

DAVID R. COLLINS

Grandfather Woo Goes to School

Read *Grandfather Woo Goes to School*. Poor David! He's only 12—well, he's only had 12 birthdays. Imagine that. He was born on leap day. He's not embarrassed about it. But he does know that children are sometimes embarrassed by different experiences. Willy was embarrassed by his grandfather's blindness. He didn't realize that his grandfather was a hero.

Write a story about the last time you were embarrassed. Maybe you'll realize it wasn't so bad after all. Use the lines below to write ideas for your rough draft.

_____
title

_____

_____

_____

_____

_____

_____

_____

Name _____ Date _____

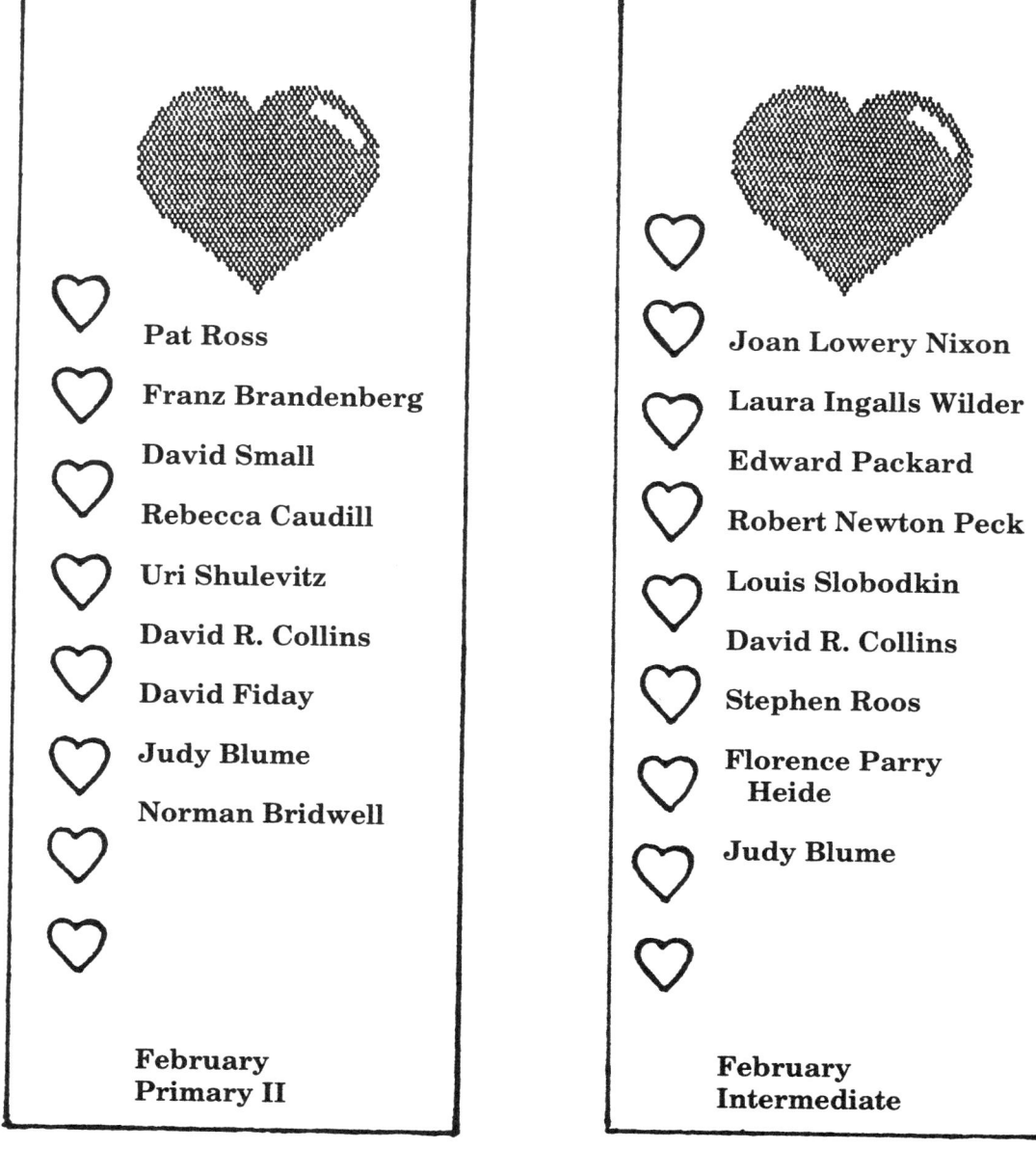

♡ Russell Hoban
♡ Dick Gackenbach
♡ Stephen Gammell
♡ Jane Yolen
♡ Mike Thaler
♡ Wilhelm Grimm
♡ Judith Viorst
♡ True Kelley
   as Kelly Oechsli
♡

**February
Primary I**

♡ Pat Ross
♡ Franz Brandenberg
♡ David Small
♡ Rebecca Caudill
♡ Uri Shulevitz
♡ David R. Collins
♡ David Fiday
♡ Judy Blume
♡ Norman Bridwell

**February
Primary II**

♡ Joan Lowery Nixon
♡ Laura Ingalls Wilder
♡ Edward Packard
♡ Robert Newton Peck
♡ Louis Slobodkin
♡ David R. Collins
♡ Stephen Roos
♡ Florence Parry Heide
♡ Judy Blume

**February
Intermediate**

FEBRUARY ANSWER KEY

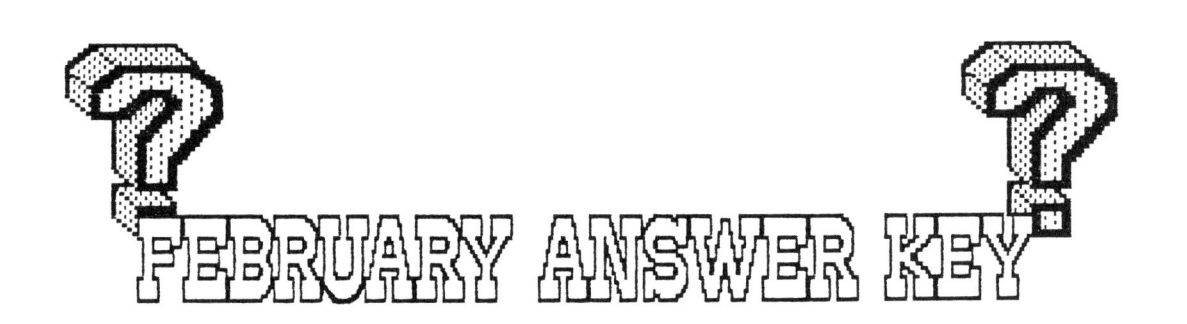

Rebecca Caudill: *A Certain Small Shepherd*

1. born, died
2. talk
3. corn
4. birds
5. fences
6. school
7. play
8. coat
9. church
10. snowstorm
11. house
12. baby, spoke

Franz Brandenberg: "The Scare" from *Leo and Emily's Big Ideas*

1. scare
2. tree
3. ring
4. telephone
5. scary
6. scarecrow
7. suit
8. hat
9. angry
10. old
11. grandmother
12. mirror

True Kelley as Kelly Oechsli: *Mice at Bat*

Answers will vary but may include the following:

Mice do not clean up ball parks, practice baseball, talk (especially to cats).

Mice do not write letters or read, ride skateboards, bat 12 at a time.

Cats do not talk (especially to mice), umpire baseball games.

Henry Wadsworth Longfellow: *Hiawatha*

1. wigwam
2. pine
3. Hiawatha
4. bear
5. stars
6. spirits
7. candle
8. flowers
9. talk
10. birds
11. language
12. secrets
13. brothers

February Answer Key

Henry Wadsworth Longfellow: "Jemima"

    do; cryin'; ears

    Poems will vary.

Uri Shulevitz: *The Magician*

1. ragged
2. tricks
3. ribbons
4. poor
5. wine
6. guest
7. neighbors
8. candlesticks
9. table
10. benches
11. appeared
12. evil, Elijah

FEBRUARY AUTHORS BIBLIOGRAPHY

February 2   Rebecca Caudill

Pocketful of Cricket (Holt, 1964)—1965 Caldecott Honor Book; *A Certain Small Shepherd* (Holt, 1965); *Wind, Sand, & Sky* (Dutton, 1976)

February 2   Judith Viorst

The Tenth Good Thing About Barney (Atheneum, 1971); *Alexander & the Terrible, Horrible, No Good, Very Bad Day* (Macmillan, 1972); *My Mama Says There Aren't Any Zombies, Ghosts, Creatures, Demons, Monsters, Fiends, Goblins, or Things* (Macmillan, 1973); *Alexander Who Used to Be Rich Last Sunday* (Macmillan, 1978); *If I Were in Charge of the World & Other Worries* (Macmillan, 1984)

February 10   Franz Brandenberg

All published by Greenwillow Books: *Nice New Neighbors* (1977); *Leo and Emily* (1981); *Leo and Emily's Big Ideas* (1982); *Leo and Emily & the Dragon* (1984); *Aunt Nina and Her Nephews and Nieces* (1984); *Aunt Nina's Visit* (1984); *The Hit of the Party* (1988)

February 10   Stephen Gammell (illustrator)

Once Upon MacDonald's Farm (Macmillan, 1981); *Wake Up Bear, It's Christmas* (Lothrop, 1981); *The Story of Mr. and Mrs. Vinegar* (Lothrop, 1982); *The Relatives Came* (Bradbury, 1985); *Song and Dance Man* (Knopf, 1988)—1989 Caldecott Medal Book

February 12   David Small

Eulalie and the Hopping Head (Macmillan, 1982); *Imogene's Antlers* (Crown, 1985); *Paper John* (Farrar, 1987)

February 20   Mary Blount Christian

Sebastian Super Sleuth (SSS) series published by Macmillan in 1986: *SSS & the Bone to Pick Mystery; SSS & the Crummy Yummies Caper; SSS & the Hair of the Dog Mystery: SSS & the Purloined Sirloin; SSS & the Secret of the Skewered Skier; SSS & the Clumsy Cowboy; SSS & the Santa Claus Caper; Penrod's Pants* (Macmillan, 1986); *Penrod Again* (Macmillan, 1987); Sherlock Street Detectives series published by Milliken in 1989: *Mystery of the Missing Scarf; The Pet Day Mystery; The UFO Mystery*

February 25   True Kelley

Buggly Bear's Hiccup Cure (Parents, 1982); *A Valentine for Fuzzboom* (Houghton Mifflin, 1982); *Home Sweet Home* (Raintree, 1983); *Mice at Bat* (Harper, 1986); *Look Baby! Listen Baby! Do Baby!* (Dutton, 1987); *Let's Eat* (Dutton, 1989); *The Mystery of the Stranger in the Barn* (Putnam, 1990)

February 27 Henry Wadsworth Longfellow

"Jemima" from *Beastly Boys and Ghastly Girls,* collected by William Cole (World Publishing, 1964); *Hiawatha,* illustrated by Susan Jeffers (Dial, 1983); *Paul Revere's Ride* (Greenwillow, 1985)

February 27 Uri Shulevitz

Illustrator of *The Fool of the World & His Flying Ship* by Arthur Ransome (Farrar, 1968)—1969 Caldecott Award Book; *Dawn* (Farrar, 1974); *The Treasure* (Farrar, 1979)—1980 Caldecott Honor Book; *One Monday Morning* (Macmillan, 1986, paperback)

February 29 David R. Collins

Primary-level books published by Milliken: *Ride a Bed Dinosaur* (1987); *Grandfather Woo Goes to School* (1990); *The Wisest Answer* (1987); biographies for grades 3-6: *Abraham Lincoln* (Mott Media, 1976); *Linda Richards: First American Trained Nurse* (Garrard, 1973); *Charles Lindbergh: Hero Pilot* (Garrard, 1978): *George Washington Carver* (Mott Media, 1981); *Francis Scott Key* (Mott Media, 1982); *Florence Nightingale* (Mott Media, 1985); *Johnny Appleseed* (Mott Media, 1985); *A Country Artist: A Story About Beatrix Potter* (Carolrhoda, 1989); *Harry S. Truman: People's President* (Chelsea House, 1991)

MARCH

March 1	Barbara Berger, *Grandfather Twilight* and *When the Sun Rose* (souvenir activity)
	Barbara Berger, *Gwinna* (writing activity)
March 1	Lonzo Anderson, *Two Hundred Rabbits* (crossword puzzle)
March 5	Mem Fox, *Guess What?* (writing activity)
March 6	Thacher Hurd, *Mama Don't Allow* (songs)
March 6	Kathleen Hague, *Bear Hugs* (writing activity)
March 11	Wanda Gag, *Millions of Cats* (writing activity)
March 11	Ezra Jack Keats, *Goggles* (word meanings)*
March 13	Ellen Raskin, *Nothing Ever Happens on My Block* (my neighborhood)
March 17	Lilian Moore, *See My Lovely Poison Ivy* (icky ingredients)
March 18	Douglas Florian, *Turtle Day* (writing activity)
March 28	Byrd Baylor, *I'm in Charge of Celebrations* (diary activity)*
March 30	Charles Keller, *Tongue Twisters* (writing activity)

March Bookmarks
March Answer Key
March Authors Bibliography

*Denotes multicultural title/activity

MARCH AUTHORS

DATE	NAME	AUTHOR	ILLUSTRATOR	K	1	2	3
1	Barbara Berger	X	X	X	X	X	X
1	Lonzo Anderson	X		X	X	X	
2	Leo Dillon		X				
2	Dr. Seuss	X	X	X	X	X	X
5	Mem Fox	X		X	X	X	
6	Kathleen Hague	X		X	X	X	
6	Thacher Hurd	X	X	X	X	X	
8	Edna Miller	X		X	X	X	
10	Jack Kent	X	X	X	X	X	
11	Wanda Gag	X	X	X	X	X	
11	Ezra Jack Keats	X	X	X	X	X	
13	Ellen Raskin	X	X	X	X	X	
13	Diane Dillon		X				
16	Sid Fleishman	X				X	X
17	Lilian Moore	X			X	X	X
17	Kate Greenaway		X	X	X	X	X
18	Douglas Florian	X	X	X	X	X	
20	Mitsumasa Anno	X	X	X	X		
21	Margaret Mahy	X		X	X	X	
22	Randolph Caldecott		X				
22	Harry Devlin	X	X	X	X	X	
24	Mary Stolz	X		X	X	X	
26	Robert Frost	X			X	X	
28	Byrd Baylor	X		X	X	X	X
30	Charles Keller	X			X	X	X

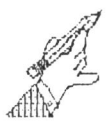

BARBARA BERGER

Grandfather Twilight ; When the Sun Rose

NOTE TO THE TEACHER: Barbara Berger's books are my favorite. They offer a very special glimpse of the world. Therefore they deserve a very special activity. I call it a souvenir activity.

Before reading *Grandfather Twilight,* go to a craft store to purchase pearl-like beads and elastic thread or gold-colored thread. Make a necklace or bracelet for each of your children. When you have read *Grandfather Twilight,* give each child a souvenir. Although this is especially effective with Kindergarten, first and second graders respond equally well. Even third graders seeing the souvenirs remember how lucky they were when they were younger.

Ask the children to retell the story in their own words. If they are like me, they will never again be able to look at twilight as just another part of the day.

Before reading *When the Sun Rose,* go to a craft store to purchase yellow fabric roses of a very small size. They usually range from eight-nine to ninety-nine cents for a dozen. If you feel like splurging, purchase a large bouquet of yellow silk roses. Place them in a vase somewhere in the room before the children arrive. It will cause curiosity to rear its nosy head.

After you read *When the Sun Rose,* give each child a small rose. As our youngest listeners are still in the concrete phase, this souvenir will help them remember the plot. As they hold their roses, ask them several questions about the story or ask them to retell the story in their own words.

BARBARA BERGER
Gwinna

NOTE TO THE TEACHER: At last, a Barbara Berger book for older, more able readers. I recommend third graders. *Gwinna* is a fairy tale reminiscent of Rapunzel. But it has all the elements of nature that Barbara Berger loves. As with her earlier picture books, Barbara's *Gwinna* deserves special activities.

Before reading *Gwinna,* read *Rapunzel* to the class. Do research to find interesting facts about owls, griffins, and harps. Have children publish their facts in a class book.

Find a very large feather and hang it over your desk or in a corner. Find a miniature tree and harp. Read *Gwinna* yourself and select other concrete objects from the story and place them around the room.

Read one chapter a day or two if you have the time. I know the children will want to reach the end of the story as soon as possible, but draw it out for the sake of enjoying the language. After you read each day, ask the children if they would like to bring to school any objects that they think about as you read the story.

After you have read *Gwinna,* have the children retell the tale in their own words. Help the children reproduce *Gwinna* as a play.

Above all, enjoy *Gwinna,* the pictures, the ideas, messages, and the language. For an insight into Barbara, read the dedication.

LONZO ANDERSON
Two Hundred Rabbits

Read *Two Hundred Rabbits*. Fill in the crossword puzzle. Use the words from the Word Bank below.

ACROSS CLUES
 3. cutting instrument
 5. leafy green vegetable
 6. magical
 8. house with straw roof
10. very big party
12. stringed instrument with bow

DOWN CLUES
 1. toss and catch in air
 2. instrument to make clear, shrill sounds
 4. watery fence
 7. stone house for King
 9. hopping furry animals
11. make pretty music with mouth

Word Bank

CASTLE	JUGGLE	RABBITS
COTTAGE	KNIFE	SING
ENCHANTED	LETTUCE	VIOLIN
FESTIVAL	MOAT	WHISTLE

Name _____ Date _____

MEM FOX

Guess What?

Read *Guess What?* But read the pictures too! Vivienne Goodman has some very strange elements in her pictures! Use the pictures to answer the following questions. Start with the picture of Daisy sleeping in bed.

1. How tall is Daisy? _____

2. What animals try to bathe with her? _____

3. What animals does she hang out to dry? _____

4. What animals are sitting on the cow? _____

5. What animal does the owl chase? _____

6. What storybook character sits on her clothes closet? _____

7. What does her owl eat? _____

8. What kind of puree does she buy? _____

9. What kind of pickles does she buy? _____

10. Where does she keep her broomstick? _____

11. What animals fly with her? _____

12. What animal is usually around her neck? _____

13. How does the storyteller know Daisy is not mean? _____
_____

Name _____ **Date** _____

THACHER HURD

Mama Don't Allow

NOTE TO THE TEACHER: Read *Mama Don't Allow*. I wish I could sing! If you can't either, find a recording or ask your music teacher to make a recording of the sheet music on the last page of the book. If you can play the piano or know someone who can, you are in business.

Have the children follow Thacher's advice from the last page. They can write verse to sing along with the music. They can use the lines below for a rough draft of their verses.

Use rules of the home, classroom, or the media center as a place to start.

Example:

Teacher don't allow no loud talkin' round here.
Teacher don't allow no loud talkin' round here.
Now we don't care what teacher don't allow.
We're gonna talk loud anyhow.
Teacher don't allow no loud talkin' round here.
Well now.

_____

_____

_____

_____

_____

Name _____ Date _____

KATHLEEN HAGUE

Bear Hugs

Read *Bear Hugs*. Kathleen loves bears and so does Michael Hague. You can hear it in her poems and see it in his pictures. But teddy bears aren't the only way we get hugs.

We can have doggie hugs, kitty cat hugs, mommie hugs, daddie hugs, and grandma and grandpa hugs. They are all special in their own way. Write about the different hugs we can get. Use the lines below for your rough draft. How about lizard or monkey hugs for people who like lizards and monkeys?

Here are two examples:

Daddie's Hug

Daddie hugs as strong as a bear.
Though on his head there is little hair,
the little whiskers on his cheeks
make my little cheeks red for weeks.

Mommie's hug

Mommie's hug is soft and sweet
as she lifts me off my feet.
As she sets me on my toes,
my small cheeks smell like a rose.

Now it's your turn!

_____

_____

_____

_____

_____

Name _____ Date _____

WANDA GAG

Millions of Cats

Read *Millions of Cats*. The old man and the old lady were lonely. They thought a cat would be nice to have around the house. But millions of cats are a different story! If your house is too quiet, what would you like to have millions of? Fill in the blanks below to help you write a story about your millions of Something or Whatever.

My backyard was so quiet the other day, I wished I had a _____.

When I heard a sound in the garage, I went to see what was happening. Boy, was I surprised to find a bunch of _____

One _____ isn't bad. Even two would be fun. But there were _____ here and there. There were _____ everywhere. There were hundreds of _____, thousands of _____, millions and billions and trillions of _____.

What would I do with all of them? They eat _____ and I didn't have enough. They like to _____ and my mom and dad wouldn't like that at all.

I couldn't keep them in my room. But I could take them to _____. Or I could _____.

But how would I ever be able to do that?

Write the story of how you solved your problem on the back of this page.

Name _____ Date _____

EZRA JACK KEATS

<u>Goggles</u>

Read *Goggles*. Write the words next to their meaning. The words in the Word Bank will help you.

1. _ _ _ _ _ _ _   protects eyes
2. _ _ _ _ _ _ _   secret place
3. _ _ _ _ _   place to live
4. _ _ _ _   belongs to me
5. _ _ _ _   closed hand
6. _ _ _ _   long hollow tube
7. _ _ _ _   sneak a look
8. _ _ _ _ _   crawled

Word Bank

crept	fist	goggles	hideout
house	mine	peek	pipe

Name _____   Date _____

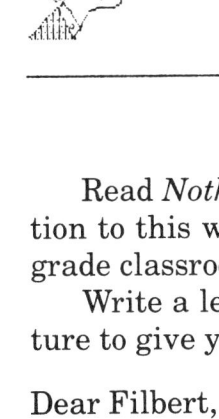

ELLEN RASKIN

Nothing Ever Happens on My Block

Read *Nothing Ever Happens on My Block*. Chester Filbert is NOT paying attention to this world. He misses enough excitement to keep a whole 1st, 2nd, or 3rd grade classroom happy for a month of Sundays.

Write a letter to Filbert telling him all the excitement he missed. Use the picture to give you clues.

Dear Filbert,

   Guess what you missed. I saw _____

_____

_____

_____

_____

_____

_____

_____

Sincerely,

Name _____ **Date** _____

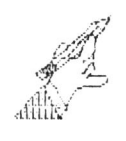

LILIAN MOORE

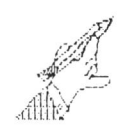

See My Lovely Poison Ivy

Read "Witch Goes Shopping" from *See My Lovely Poison Ivy*. Lilian Moore's witch friend has a terrible time finding certain witch ingredients for her special potions.

Name ten other ingredients a witch couldn't find at your local grocery store.

Here are two examples:

SWAMP THINGS WINGS   RATTLESNAKE FANGS

Now It's your turn!

_____

_____

_____

_____

_____

_____

_____

Name _____   Date _____

DOUGLAS FLORIAN

<u>Turtle Day</u>

Read *Turtle Day*. Do you think Douglas like turtles? I do. But I wish he would have written a book about bunnies. I love BUNNIES! Maybe you could write a story for me. But I do like cats, too, and monkeys, and elephants, and lizards and. . . oh well. I like all kinds of animals. Probably the one you love, too!

Pick an animal you love and write a story about its day. Draw the pictures, too. Share it with a friend. The lines below are for your rough draft ideas.

_____ Day

_____

_____

_____

_____

_____

_____

_____

Name _____   Date _____

BYRD BAYLOR

I'm in Charge of Celebrations

Read *I'm in Charge of Celebrations*. Just as the young girl saves her special days on paper, we can too. If you don't have a diary or journal, start one TODAY! They are great for looking back and seeing what you thought was important long ago. It helps you see that bad times pass. Sadness can be forgotten. It also shows you that we can forget exciting days if we don't write them down.

To start your "Celebration Journal," write down something wonderful or simple that happened to you today, this week, or last week. It may not be wonderful to everyone. It doesn't need to be. It just has to be special to you. Here are two entries from my "Celebration Journal."

We have a new reader in the world today. Adam is in Kindergarten and he knows his word list—so here he goes. I really love helping Kindergarten children find books they can read. Next year they'll be taking home one book a day from a set of 150 books I have ordered especially for them. Our children start reading earlier and earlier every year. I just hope I can keep a large stock of great books for them. But I know I will—because that is my JOB!! And I love it.

♡ ♡ ♡

I thought I was going to actually die today. Joey has been struggling with his reading for almost two years. We haven't given up on him and most important, he hasn't given up on himself. He read *Time to Go* today—my book. I remember when he was in Kindergarten. Now he's reading my book in second grade. I'm not only proud, I'm happy for him, because he is reading my book. I'm not reading it to him.

Get busy writing your celebrations!

Name _____ Date _____

CHARLES KELLER
Tongue Twisters

Read *Tongue Twisters*. Tongue twisters are fun to say and fun to write. Use the lines below to write phrases or sentences that begin with the same sound.

Tongue twisters can be strings of works like:

rubber baby bumpers

or tiny stories or ideas like:

Sally sells seashells by the seashore.

How much wood would a woodchuck chuck
if a woodchuck could chuck wood.

Peter Piper picked a peck of pickled peppers.
If Peter Piper picked a peck of pickled peppers,
where is the peck of pickled peppers
that Peter Piper picked?

Use the lines below to write your own tongue twisters. Share them with the children in your class.

_____

_____

_____

_____

_____

Name _____ **Date** _____

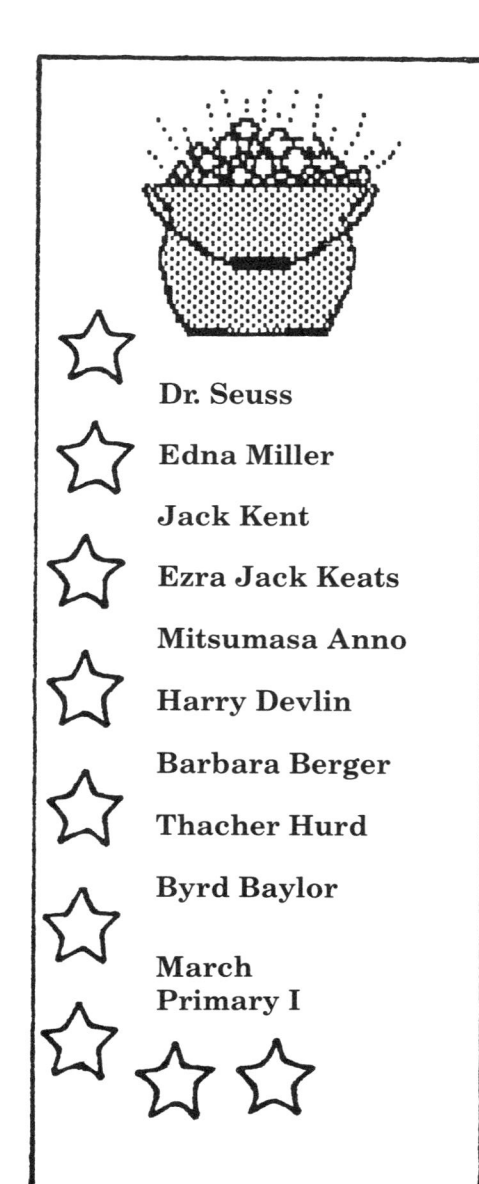

Bookmark 1

☆ Dr. Seuss
☆ Edna Miller
☆ Jack Kent
☆ Ezra Jack Keats
☆ Mitsumasa Anno
☆ Harry Devlin
☆ Barbara Berger
☆ Thacher Hurd
☆ Byrd Baylor

March
Primary I
☆
☆

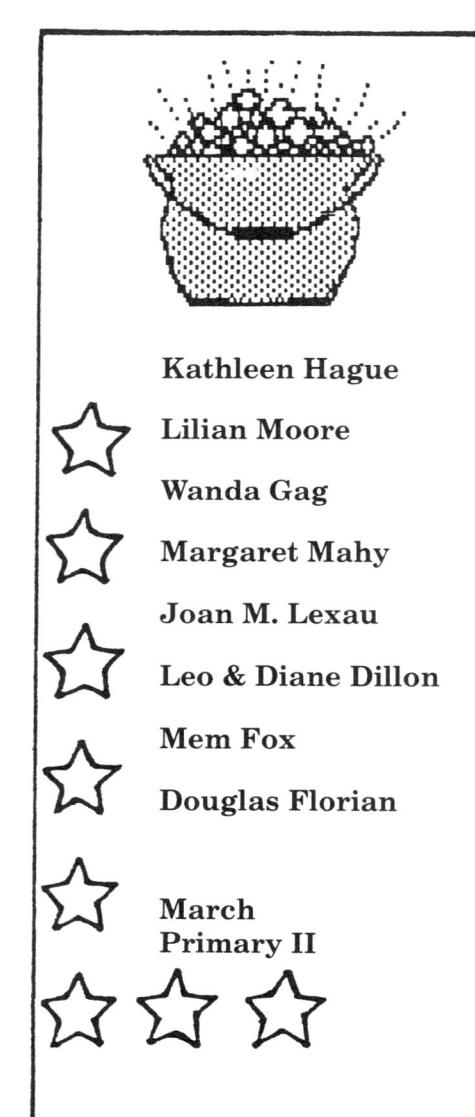

Bookmark 2

Kathleen Hague ☆
Lilian Moore ☆
Wanda Gag
Margaret Mahy ☆
Joan M. Lexau ☆
Leo & Diane Dillon ☆
Mem Fox ☆
Douglas Florian ☆

March
Primary II
☆
☆

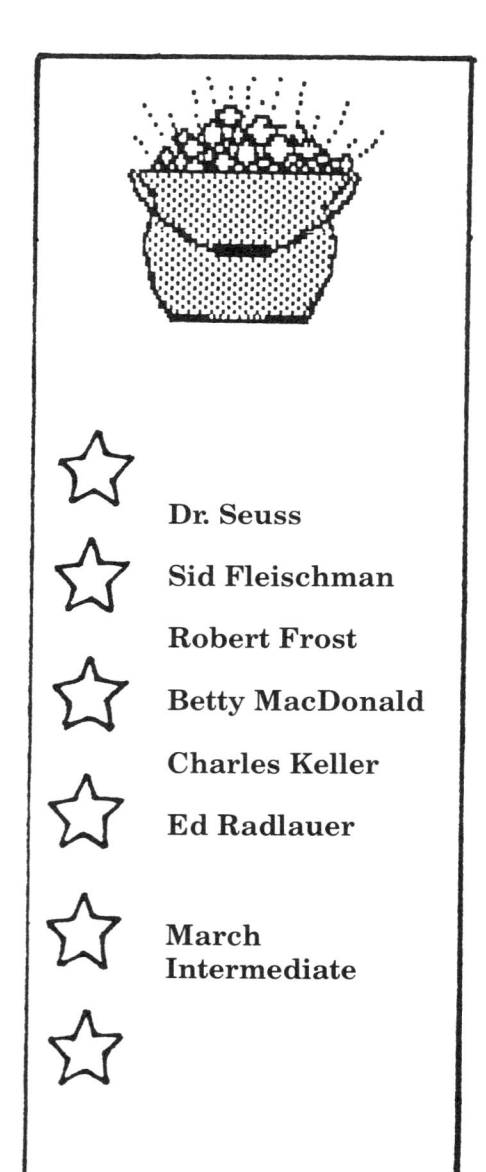

Bookmark 3

☆ Dr. Seuss
☆ Sid Fleischman
☆ Robert Frost
☆ Betty MacDonald
☆ Charles Keller
☆ Ed Radlauer

March
Intermediate

MARCH ANSWER KEY

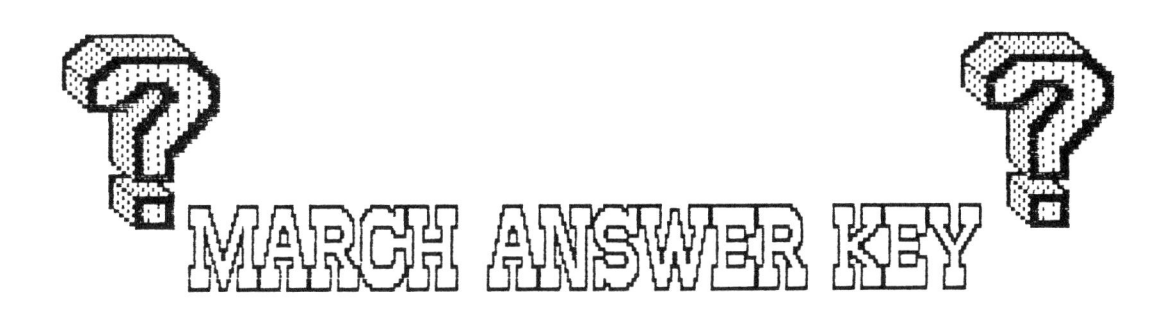

Lonzo Anderson: *Two Hundred Rabbits*

Across

3. knife
5. lettuce
6. enchanted
8. cottage
10. festival
12. violin

Down

1. juggle
2. whistle
4. moat
7. castle
9. rabbits
11. sing

Mem Fox: *Guess What?*

1. 5 feet, 11¾ inches
2. fish, frog, miniature whale tail in the sink
3. fish, spider
4. owl, frog
5. black cat
6. Max from *Where the Wild Things Are*
7. mice
8. lizard's liver
9. mucus
10. by the outhouse
11. bat on her hat, fox around her neck
12. fox or snake
13. Answers will vary. One possible answer is that she's laughing, perhaps at us, because every answer in the text so far has been "yes," but now the last answer is "no." She's a tricky witch.

Ezra Jack Keats: *Goggles*

1. goggles
2. hideout
3. house
4. mine
5. fist
6. pipe
7. peek
8. crept

MARCH AUTHORS BIBLIOGRAPHY

March 1 Barbara Berger
Animalia (Celestial Arts, 1982); *The Donkey's Dream* (Putnam, 1986); *When the Sun Rose* (Philomel, 1986); *Grandfather Twilight* (Philomel, 1988); *Gwinna* (Philomel, 1990)

March 1 Lonzo Anderson
Two Hundreds Rabbits (Viking, 1968)—out of print

March 5 Mem Fox
Wilfrid Gordon MacDonald Partridge (Kane Miller, 1985); *Arabella, Smallest Girl in the World* (Scholastic, 1987); *Possum Magic* (Abingdon, 1987); *Guess What?* (HBJ, 1988); *Hattie and the Fox* (Bradbury, 1988); *With Love at Christmas* (Abingdon, 1988)

March 6 Thacher Hurd
He is the son of the Caldecott author/illustrator writing team of Edith Thacher Hurd and Clement Hurd. *Axle the Freeway Cat* (Harper, 1981); *Hobo Dog* (Scholastic, 1981); *Mystery on the Docks* (Harper, 1983); *Mama Don't Allow* (Harper, 1984); *Hobo Dog in the Ghost Town* (Scholastic, 1986); *Pea Patch Jig* (Crown, 1986)

March 6 Kathleen Hague
All illustrated by Michael Hague: *East of the Sun, West of the Moon* (HBJ, 1980); *Man Who Kept House* (HBJ, 1981); *Alphabears* (Holt, 1985); *Legend of the Veery Bird* (HBJ, 1985); *Numbears* (Holt, 1986); *Out of the Nursery, Into the Night* (Holt, 1986); *Bear Hugs* (Holt, 1989)

March 11 Wanda Gag
ABC Bunny (Putnam, 1933); *Snow White and the Seven Dwarfs* (Coward, 1938)—1939 Caldecott Honor Book; *Nothing at All* (Coward, 1941)—1942 Caldecott Honor Book; *Funny Thing* (Putnam, 1960); *Gone Is Gone* (Putnam, 1960); *Millions of Cats* (Putnam, 1977); *Jorinda and Joringel,* coauthored with Margot Tomes (Putnam, 1979); *The Sorcerer's Apprentice,* coauthored with Margot Tomes (Putnam, 1979); *The Earth Gnome* (Putnam, 1985)

March 11 Ezra Jack Keats
The Snowy Day (Viking, 1962)—1963 Caldecott Book; *Whistle for Willie* (Viking Penguin, 1964); *Goggles* (Macmillan, 1969)—1970 Caldecott Book; *Kitten for a Day* (Macmillan, 1974); *The Trip* (Greenwillow, 1978); *Louie's Search* (Macmillan, 1980); *Clementina's Cactus* (Viking Penguin, 1982); *Louie* (Greenwillow, 1983); *Peter's Chair* (Harper, 1983); *Jennie's Hat* (Harper, 1985); *Apartment Three* (Macmillan, 1986); *Little Drummer Boy* (Macmillan,

1987); *Maggie and the Pirate* (Macmillan, 1987); *Pet Show!* (Macmillan, 1987); *Hi, Cat!*, second edition (Macmillan, 1988)

March 13 Ellen Raskin
Ghost in a Four Room Apartment (Macmillan, 1978); *Spectacles* (Macmillan, 1988); *Nothing Ever Happens on My Block* (Macmillan, 1989)

March 17 Lilian Moore
The Riddle Walk (Garrard, 1971); *See My Lovely Poison Ivy* (Atheneum, 1975); *I Feel the Same Way* (Macmillan, 1976); *Go with the Poem* (McGraw, 1979); *Something New Begins* (Macmillan, 1982); *The Magic Spectacles and Other Easy to Read Stories* (Bantam, 1985); *Little Raccoon's Nighttime Adventure* (Western, 1986)

March 18 Douglas Florian
People Working (Crowell, 1983); *Discovering Frogs* (Macmillan, 1986); *Discovering Seashells* (Macmillan, 1986); *A Winter Day* (Greenwillow, 1987); *A Summer Day* (Greenwillow, 1988); *Turtle Day* (Crowell, 1989); *A Year in the Country* (Greenwillow, 1989); *Discovering Butterflies* (Macmillan, 1990); *Discovering Trees* (Macmillan, 1990)

March 28 Byrd Baylor
All published by Macmillan: *Desert Voices* (1981); *If You Are a Hunter of Fossils* (1984); *Everybody Needs a Rock* (1985); *Guess Who My Favorite Person Is?* (1985); *Best Town in the World* (1986); *The Desert Is Theirs* (1986); *Hawk, I am Your Brother* (1986); *I'm in Charge of Celebrations* (1986); *The Way to Start a Day* (1986); *When Clay Sings* (1987); *Amigo* (1989)

March 30 Charles Keller
He is the world's greatest collector of jokes, riddles, and puns. All published by Prentice Hall: *Giggle Puss: Pet Jokes for Kids* (1977); *Still Going Bananas* (1980); *School Daze* (1981); *Smokey the Shark: And Other Fishy Stories* (1981); *Alexander the Grape: Fruit and Vegetable Jokes* (1982); *Oh, Brother: And Other Family Jokes* (1982); *Ohm on the Range: Robot and Computer Jokes* (1982); *Little Witch Presents a Monster Joke Book* (1983); *Remember the a la Mode! Riddles and Puns* (1983); *Grime Doesn't Pay: Law and Order Jokes* (1984); *What's Up, Doc? Doctor and Dentist Jokes* (1984); *Astronuts: Space Jokes and Riddles* (1985); *Count Draculations! Monster Riddles* (1986); *Waiter, There's a Fly in My Soup* (1986); *Tongue Twisters* (Simon and Schuster, 1989); *King Henry the Ape: Animal Jokes* by Edward Frascino, compiled by Charles Keller (Pippin Press, 1990)

APRIL

April 1	Jan Wahl, *Humphrey's Bear* (favorite toy activity)
April 2	Peter Collington, *The Angel and the Soldier Boy; On Christmas Eve* (writing a story)
April 7	Tony Palazzo, *Timothy Turtle* (rhyming words)
April 8	Ruth Chew, *No Such Thing as a Witch* (booklet)
April 8	Trina Schart Hyman, *Little Red Riding Hood* (fill in)
April 9	Nigel Gray, *A Country Far Away* (country research)*
April 10	Clare Turlay Newberry, *April's Kittens* (writing activity)
April 22	Kurt Wiese, *Fish in the Air* (fill in/drawing activity)*
April 22	Eileen Christelow, *Five Little Monkeys Jumping on the Bed* (song writing)
April 25	Alvin Schwartz, *In a Dark, Dark Room and Other Scary Stories* (sound effects)
April 29	Edith Baer, *This Is the Way We Go to School* (writing activity)*
April 29	Nicole Rubel, *Uncle Henry and Aunt Henrietta's Honeymoon* (exaggeration dialogue)
April 30	Maria Leach, *The Thing at the Foot of the Bed* (writing activity)

April Bookmarks
April Answer Key
April Authors Bibliography

*Denotes multicultural title/activity

APRIL AUTHORS

DATE	NAME	AUTHOR/ILLUSTRATOR		READING LEVEL			
				K	1	2	3
1	Jan Wahl	X	X	X	X		
2	Peter Collington	X	X	X	X	X	
2	Hans Christian Andersen	X				X	X
3	Washington Irving	X					X
4	Elizabeth Levy	X				X	X
7	Tony Palazzo	X	X	X	X	X	
7	Donald Carrick	X	X			X	X
8	Ruth Chew	X				X	X
8	Trina Schart Hyman		X				
9	Nigel Gray	X	X	X	X	X	
10	Clare T. Newberry	X	X	X	X	X	
10	David Adler	X				X	X
12	C. W. Anderson	X			X	X	
12	Beverly Cleary	X		X	X	X	
16	Gertrude Chandler Warner	X				X	X
22	Kurt Wiese	X				X	X
22	Eileen Christelow	X	X	X	X	X	
24	Evaline Ness	X	X			X	X
25	Alvin Schwartz					X	X
26	Patricia Reilly Giff	X				X	X
27	Wende Devlin	X				X	X
27	Ludwig Bemelmans	X	X	X	X	X	
27	John Burningham	X	X	X	X		
29	Nicole Rubel	X	X	X	X	X	
29	Edith Baer	X		X	X	X	X
30	Maria Leach	X					X

JAN WAHL

Humphrey's Bear

Read *Humphrey's Bear*. Use the words in the Word Bank to finish these sentences about Humphrey's nighttime adventure with a stuffed bear.

1. When is a person too _____ to sleep with a bear?
2. Humphrey _____ into bed.
3. The bear belonged to Humphrey's _____ long ago.
4. Humphrey's bear gave him a _____.
5. They went for a _____ in a _____.
6. There was a _____ in the back _____.
7. Humphrey's bear told him to _____.
8. They drank cups of hot _____.
9. Humphrey's bear played the _____.
10. A _____ came up suddenly.
11. Humphrey found his bear on an _____.
12. Dad remembered _____ with Humphrey too.

Word Bank							
banjo	boat	cap	chocolate	father	island	old	
ride	river	sailing	snuggled	steer	typhoon	yard	

Name _____   Date _____

PETER COLLINGTON

The Angel and the Soldier Boy; On Christmas Eve

Look at the pictures in *The Angel and the Soldier Boy* and *On Christmas Eve*. Peter Collington is an excellent storyteller with pictures.

Write a story to go with one of Peter's books. Type or print your story neatly on 3 × 5 inch self-stick notes. When the story is done, place the notes on the correct page. Now the story is written by you and illustrated by Peter Collington. You two make a great author/illustrator team. Share your story with your classmates.

Use the lines below to gather ideas about the sentences you will use.

_____

_____

_____

_____

_____

_____

_____

Name _____   Date _____

TONY PALAZZO
Timothy Turtle

Read *Timothy Turtle* by Al Graham, illustrated by Tony Palazzo. This Caldecott Honor book is filled with rhyming words. Use the words in the Word Bank to write the words that rhyme with the listed words.

1. lake _____ _____
2. fun _____ _____
3. led _____ _____
4. hill _____ _____
5. along _____ _____
6. spies _____ _____
7. me _____
8. played _____ _____ _____
9. quit _____ _____
10. space _____ _____
11. in _____ _____

Word Bank

admit	agree	bit	bun	cries	dismayed	face
fade	grade	make	none	pill	place	read
said	song	spin	surprise	take	thrill	win

Name _____ Date _____

RUTH CHEW

No Such Thing as a Witch

NOTE TO THE TEACHER:

Many authors offer children an entire series of books with repeating characters. Through the years, children enjoy reading all of them. You may be one of these series lovers yourself. In order to support the idea of reading a series, I use a software program called *Print Shop*. One component of that software produces greeting cards. The Ruth Chew booklet on the following page is an example of the program's ability. If you have a computer with a printer or have access to one, you can make series booklets for a variety of authors.

The outside of the card is produced with the software. The title listing on the inside is typed with a typewriter. You may also type the list on the computer, cut it out, and paste it in the appropriate area.

To use the Ruth Chew booklet, simply fold it like a greeting card, in half and in half again. Now the children can check off the titles as they read them.

Another idea for the software program is to produce a booklet entitled "Books I Love" and have the children write the names of the books they read on the inside. As soon as it is filled, they can start another. Some teachers even let the children design their own booklets. The software is simple to operate and simple to understand.

BEWITCHING!

Place an X in front of the titles you have read.

Other witch titles by Ruth Chew:

____ *Do-It-Yourself Magic*
____ *Earthstar Magic*
____ *Magic Cave*
____ *The Magic Coin*
____ *Mostly Magic*
____ *Second-Hand Magic*
____ *Summer Magic*
____ *The Trouble with Magic*
____ *What the Witch Left*
____ *The Witch at the Window*
____ *Witch in the House*
____ *The Would-Be Witch*

READ ANOTHER
RUTH CHEW
BOOK
IF
YOU
DARE!

THEY ARE . . .

NIGEL GRAY

A Country Far Away

    Read *A Country Far Away*. This story shows how similar lives can be. We all stay home once in a while, help mon and dad, new brothers and sisters, play games, ride bikes, go to school, and have visits from cousins. We can also plan to visit a country we have read about.

    What country would you visit if you could go on a trip? Have you ever been to a different country? Canada? Mexico?

    I would like to visit Germany because my grandparents came from there. I would like to see the castles, the Rhine river, and a large cathedral. I would like to visit a school and hear the Kindergarten children say the alphabet and sing nursery rhymes. I would like to hear a first or second grade teacher read *Little Red Riding Hood* or *Hansel and Gretel*. I would like to hear people speak German and hear how they laugh. Do you think they laugh the same as we do? Do you think they smile like we do? There are wonderful things to learn in a foreign country.

    Write about a country that you would like to visit. What would you like to see and do? Use the lines below to write a few things you would see and do. Go to the media center and find a book about that country. Discover the answers to all your questions.

_____

_____

_____

_____

_____

_____

Name _____ **Date** _____

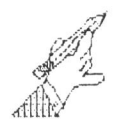

TRINA SCHART HYMAN

Little Red Riding Hood

Read *Little Red Riding Hood*. Use the words in the Word Bank to finish these sentences about a little girl who escapes from the Big Bad Wolf!

1. Elizabeth loved her little red _____.

2. One day, her grandmother was _____.

3. Her mother filled a _____ with bread, butter, and wine.

4. She told Little Red to stay on the _____.

5. She warned her daughter not to _____.

6. Little Red met a _____.

7. He got _____ to grandma's house.

8. He tricked her into picking some _____.

9. Meanwhile, the wolf ate grandma in one _____.

10. Little Red was his _____.

11. The huntsman heard a much-too-loud _____.

12. He _____ open the wolf to save Little Red and grandma.

13. Little Red never _____ from the path again, as far as we know.

Word Bank						
basket	cut	daydream	dessert	directions	flowers	
gulp	hood	path	sick	snore	strayed	wolf

Name _____ Date _____

CLARE T. NEWBERRY

April's Kittens

Read *April's Kittens*. April's cat and kitten were saved when her family decided to rent a new two bedroom apartment. She was so happy, she wrote a little song in her head called *Song for Cats*.

Write your own *Song for Cats*. If you do not like cats, write a song for another animal that you keep or would like to keep as a pet. I wonder if any of you have a pet python? That's a song I would like to hear!

Use the lines below for a rough draft of your song.

_____

_____

_____

_____

_____

_____

_____

Name _____ **Date** _____

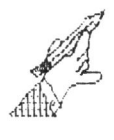

KURT WIESE

Fish in the Air

Read *Fish in the Air*. Use the words in the Word Bank to finish these sentences about a little boy's adventure with a kite.

1. Little Fish lived in _____.

2. His shoes looked like _____.

3. His father bought him a fish _____.

4. Little Fish wanted a _____.

5. His father took him to a special _____.

6. Little Fish picked the _____ kite.

7. Suddenly a Tai Fung, or _____ _____, hit.

8. Little Fish went _____ into the air.

9. A Fish _____ attacked the kite.

10. Little Fish _____ back to earth.

11. He landed in a _____.

12. Little Fish wanted a _____ fish kite.

Word Bank						
big	biggest	China	fish	floated	Hawk	kite
lantern	net	sailing	small	street	wind	

ON THE BACK OF THIS PAGE, DESIGN A KITE YOU WOULD LIKE TO FLY. COLOR IT!

Name _____   Date _____

EILEEN CHRISTELOW

Five Little Monkeys Jumping on the Bed

Read *Five Little Monkeys Jumping on the Bed.* These are some of the worst monkeys I have ever seen in a book. But since it is all in fun, let's write your own book using the idea Eileen did so well.

Write a story about children in school or... anything you want. Here's an idea you can finish.

Use the lines below to finish the rough draft or start your own.

It was time for school. Twenty-five little children walked down the hall.

They took off their coats and hung them in the locker with their lunch pails.

Twenty-five little children said "Good morning, teacher."

Then twenty-five little children started jumping on their desks.

Three fell off and bumped their heads. Teacher called the principal.

Principal said, "No more children jumping on the desks!"

_____

_____

_____

_____

_____

Name _____   Date _____

ALVIN SCHWARTZ

In a Dark, Dark Room and Other Scary Stories

Read *In a Dark, Dark Room and Other Scary Stories*. These stories are very scary. All they need is sound effects. That could be scary effects from a record, scary music, scary noises you make with your mouth, your hands, or special instruments.

Pick one story and ask your teacher to make a photocopy of it. Use red ink to show where the sound effects will go. Find enough people to help you perform it for the class. Find a room that is very dark! Have fun being scared!

Use the lines below to gather ideas for the sound effects you need.

_____

_____

_____

_____

_____

_____

_____

Name _____ **Date** _____

EDITH BAER

This Is the Way We Go to School

Read *This Is the Way We Go to School.* Most of us ride a bus, but some walk, some ride in a car. But if you live in another country or area, you could go to school in a helicopter! Wouldn't that be fun?

What would be your favorite way to travel to school? Pick one group of children to join as they go to school. Write a story about your trip with them. Think about these questions when you write.

1. What are the advantages (good points) of traveling that way?

2. What are the disadvantages (bad points) of traveling that way?

3. Do you think they always have good times traveling that way? What kinds of things could go wrong?

Go to the media center and find a book about that country. There is a map at the back of the book. Write down five facts about that country. Write your reaction to those five facts. Put your facts with the facts from children in your room to make a book. You will have a classbook on facts about countries around the world. Keep the facts about countries on the same continent together and you will have continent books.

Use the lines below to start your story of traveling with children from another state or country.

_____

_____

_____

_____

Name _____ **Date** _____

NICOLE RUBEL

Uncle Henry and Aunt Henrietta's Honeymoon

Read *Uncle Henry and Aunt Henrietta's Honeymoon*. What confusion! I don't know what really happened. The arctic? The desert? The jungle? That is the charm of this story. The exaggeration is wonderful. Let's write an exaggerated dialogue, too.

Pick a situation from home or school, a friend to talk to, and write a dialogue that hardly anyone would believe, but that everyone would enjoy. Use the lines below.

Name _____   Date _____

MARIA LEACH

The Thing at the Foot of the Bed

    Read *The Thing at the Foot of the Bed*. This book is filled with the scariest stories.

    Use the space below to draw the THING you saw at the foot of your bed. If everyone in your class does this activity, you will have a book of things. Use the lines below to name your thing, to tell where it came from, what it likes to eat, and how one gets rid of a such a thing. On another piece of paper, write a dialogue you had with your thing late one dark and gloomy night. Use additional paper if you need more room.

_____

_____

_____

Name _____ **Date** _____

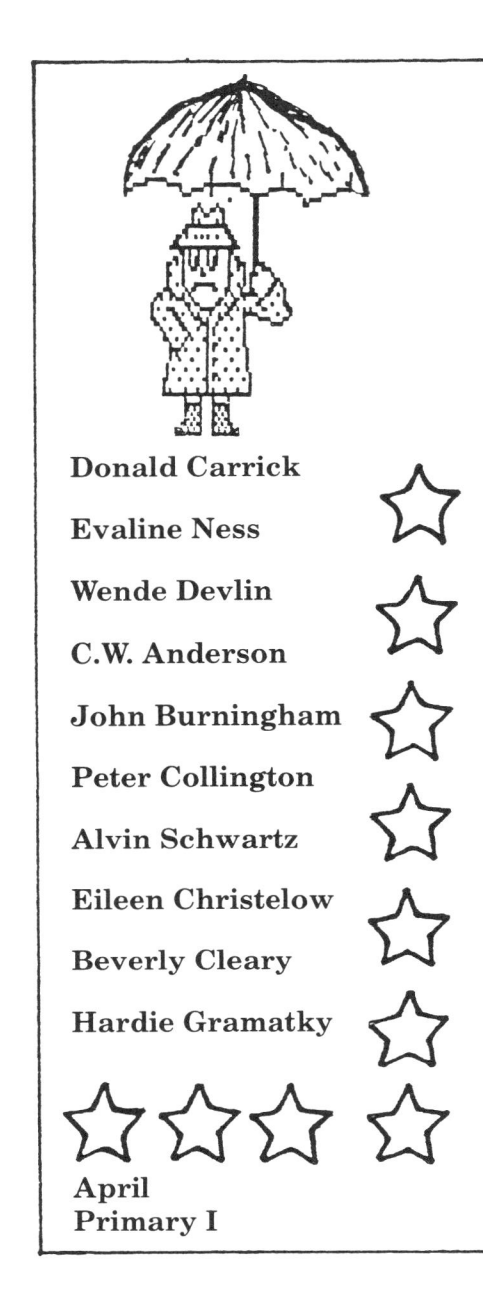

April Primary I

- Donald Carrick ☆
- Evaline Ness ☆
- Wende Devlin ☆
- C.W. Anderson ☆
- John Burningham ☆
- Peter Collington ☆
- Alvin Schwartz ☆
- Eileen Christelow ☆
- Beverly Cleary ☆
- Hardie Gramatky ☆

☆☆☆

April Primary II

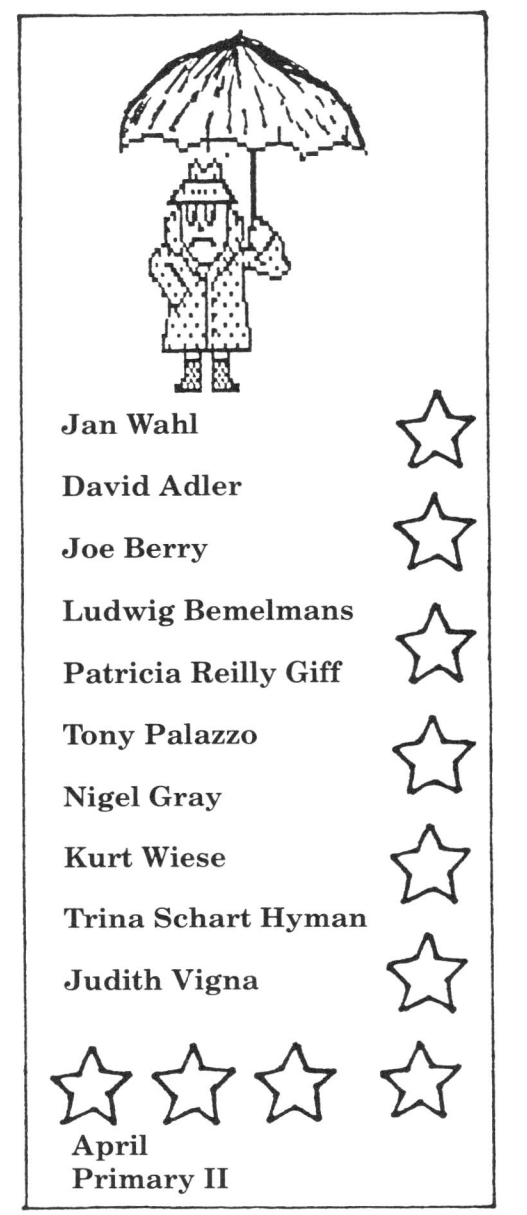

- Jan Wahl ☆
- David Adler ☆
- Joe Berry ☆
- Ludwig Bemelmans ☆
- Patricia Reilly Giff ☆
- Tony Palazzo ☆
- Nigel Gray ☆
- Kurt Wiese ☆
- Trina Schart Hyman
- Judith Vigna ☆

☆☆☆

April Intermediate

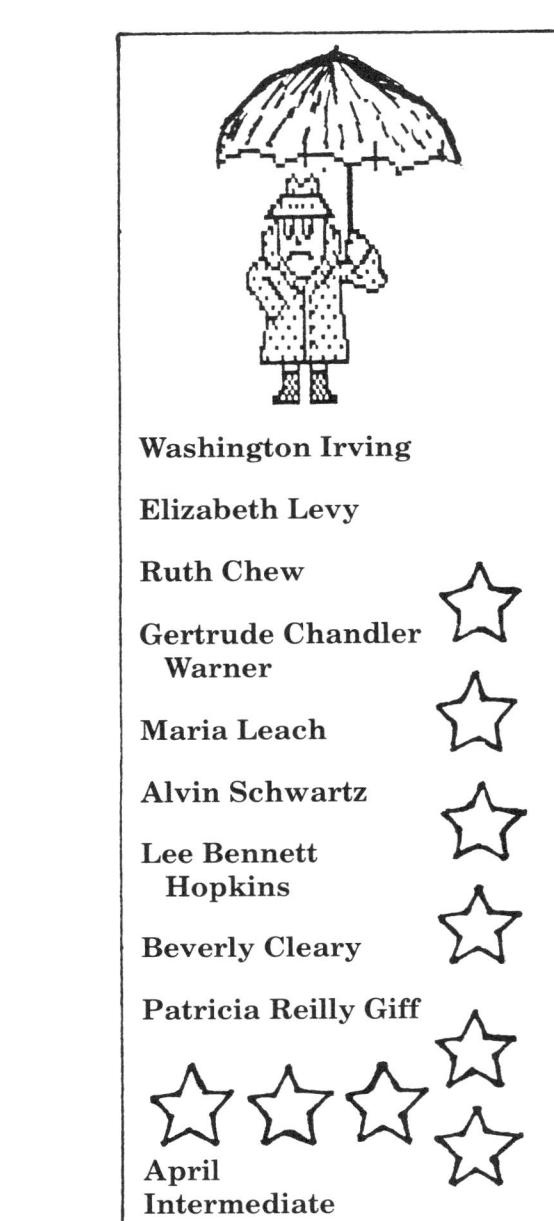

- Washington Irving
- Elizabeth Levy ☆
- Ruth Chew ☆
- Gertrude Chandler Warner ☆
- Maria Leach ☆
- Alvin Schwartz ☆
- Lee Bennett Hopkins ☆
- Beverly Cleary ☆
- Patricia Reilly Giff ☆

☆☆☆☆

APRIL ANSWER KEY

Jan Wahl: *Humphrey's Bear*

1. old
2. snuggled
3. father
4. cap
5. ride, boat
6. river, yard
7. steer
8. chocolate
9. banjo
10. typhoon
11. island
12. sailing

Tony Palazzo: *Timothy Turtle*

1. make, take
2. bun, none
3. read, said
4. pill, thrill
5. song
6. cries, surprise
7. agree
8. dismayed, fade, grade
9. admit, bit
10. face, place
11. spin, win

Trina Schart Hyman: *Little Red Riding Hood*

1. hood
2. sick
3. basket
4. path
5. daydream
6. wolf
7. directions
8. flowers
9. gulp
10. dessert
11. snore
12. cut
13. strayed

Kurt Wiese: *Fish in the Air*

1. China
2. fish
3. Lantern
4. kite
5. street
6. biggest
7. big, wind
8. sailing
9. hawk
10. floated
11. net
12. small

APRIL AUTHORS BIBLIOGRAPHY

April 1 Jan Wahl

Grandmother Told Me (Little, Brown, 1972)—out of print; *Doctor Rabbit's Foundling* (Pantheon, 1977); *Dracula's Cat* (Prentice Hall, 1981); *Tiger Watch* (HBJ, 1982); *Rabbits on Rollerskates* (Crown, 1986); *The Toy Circus* (HBJ, 1986); *Humphrey's Bear* (Holt, 1987)

April 2 Peter Collington

The Angel and the Soldier Boy (Knopf, 1987); *On Christmas Eve* (Knopf, 1990)

April 7 Tony Palazzo

Timothy Turtle (Scott Foresman, 1946)—1947 Caldecott Honor Book; *Animal Family Album* (Lion Books, 1967); *Magic Crayon* (Lion Books, 1967); *Animals of the Night* (Lion Books, 1970); *The Biggest and Littlest Animals* (Lion Books, 1973)

April 8 Ruth Chew

Enjoyable easy-reading witch series for grades 2-3, newly reprinted by Scholastic: *No Such Thing as a Witch* (1972); *Summer Magic* (1977); *Mostly Magic* (1982); *Secondhand Magic* (1982); *The Magic Coin* (1983); *Magic in the Park* (1983); *The Trouble with Magic* (1985); *The Witch at the Window* (1985); *The Would-Be Witch* (1986); *What the Witch Left* (1986)

April 8 Trina Schart Hyman

Illustrated *Saint George and the Dragon* retold by Margaret Hodges (Little, Brown, 1984)—1985 Caldecott Award Book, retold and illustrated Grimm Brothers' tales, including *Little Red Riding Hood, The Sleeping Beauty,* and *Rapunzel*

April 9 Nigel Gray

The One and Only Robin Hood (Little, Brown, 1987); *A Balloon for Grandad* (Orchard, 1988); *A Country Far Away* (Watts, 1989)

April 10 Clare Turlay Newberry

Barkis (Harper, 1938); *April's Kittens* (Harper, 1940)—1941 Caldecott Honor Book

April 22 Kurt Wiese

Fish in the Air (Viking, 1948)—1949 Caldecott Honor Book

April 22   Eileen Christelow

All published by Clarion Books: *Henry and the Red Stripes* (1982); *Henry and the Dragon* (1984); *Jerome and the Babysitter* (1985); *Mr. Murphy's Marvelous Invention* (1986); *The Robbery at the Diamond Dog Diner* (1986); *Olive and the Magic Hat* (1987); *Five Little Monkeys Jumping on the Bed* (1989); *Jerome and the Witchcraft Kids* (1990)

April 25   Alvin Schwartz

All of Alvin's books are great for reading out loud to children. Easy-to-read humor selections published by Harper, including: *Busy Buzzing Bumblebees* (1982); *All Our Noses Are Here & Other Noodle Tales* (1985); *In a Dark, Dark Room and Other Scary Stories* (1985); tall tales and superstitions also published by Harper: *Witcracks: Jokes and Jests from American Folklore* (1973); *Cross Your Fingers & Spit in Your Hat* (1974); *Whoppers: Tall Tales and Other Lies* (1975)

April 29   Edith Baer

This Is the Way We Go to School (Scholastic, 1990)

April 29   Nicole Rubel

Illustrator of the *Rotten Ralph* series (Houghton) by Jack Gantos; *Pirate Jupiter and the Moondogs* (Dial, 1985); *Uncle Henry and Aunt Henrietta's Honeymoon* (1986); *It Came from the Swamp* (Dial, 1988)

April 30   Maria Leach

The Thing at the Foot of the Bed (Dell, 1981); *Whistle in the Graveyard* (Penguin, 1982)

MAY

May 3	Mavis Jukes, *Like Jake and Me* (fill in)
May 6	Giulio Maestro, *Ferryboat* (fill in)
May 16	Bruce Coville, *Sarah's Unicorn* and *Sarah and the Dragon* (writing activity)
May 17	Eloise Greenfield, *Honey, I Love* (biographical poem)*
May 21	Phyllis Halloran, *Cat Purrs* (poetry)
May 23	Peter Parnall, *The Great Fish* (fill in)*
May 29	Brock Cole, *The Giant's Toe* (fill in)
May 30	Millicent Selsam, *Terry and the Caterpillars* (fill in)
May 31	Elaine Moore, *Mixed-Up Sam* (fill in)
May 31	Elizabeth Coatsworth, *The Cat Who Went to Heaven* (cat research)*

May Bookmarks
May Answer Key
May Authors Bibliography

*Denotes multicultural title/activity

MAY AUTHORS

DATE	NAME	AUTHOR/ILLUSTRATOR	READING LEVEL			
			K	1	2	3
3	Mavis Jukes	X				X
4	Don Wood		X	X	X	X	
5	Leo Lionni	X	X	X	X	X	
6	Judy Delton	X			X	X
6	Giulio Maestro	X	X		X	X	
7	Nonny Hogrogian	X	X	X	X	X	X
9	James Barrie	X					X
12	Edward Lear	X	X			X	X
14	George Selden	X				X	X
15	L. Frank Baum	X					X
16	Bruce Coville	X	X	X	X	X	X
17	Eloise Greenfield	X				X	X
18	Lillian Hoban	X	X	X	X	X	
19	Thomas Feelings		X				
20	Carol Carrick	X				X	X
21	Phyllis Halloran	X		X	X	X	
22	Arnold Lobel	X	X	X	X	X	X
23	Margaret Wise Brown	X		X	X	X	
23	Peter Parnall	X					X
25	Martha Alexander	X	X	X	X	X	
29	Brock Cole	X	X	X	X	X	
30	Millicent Selsam	X			X	X	X
31	Elaine Moore	X		X	X		
31	Elizabeth Coatsworth| X					X

MAVIS JUKES

Like Jake and Me

Read *Like Jake and Me*. This Newbery Honor Book shows how a stepson and stepfather conquer each other's fear—one on purpose, the other accidentally.

1. Jake didn't need help splitting _____.

2. Virginia was having _____.

3. She grew _____ in a _____.

4. Alex was taking _____ lessons.

5. Alex saw a _____ spider.

6. Jake was looking at _____.

7. Jake was _____ of spiders. Alex helped him.

8. Jake's boot knocked out Alex's loose _____.

9. Virginia found the spider on Jake's _____.

10. Alex and Jake _____ on the _____.

Word Bank

afraid	ballet	bottle	danced	hat	pears
porch	tooth	twins	Virginia	wolf	wood

Name _____ Date _____

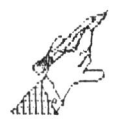

GIULIO MAESTRO

Ferryboat

Read *Ferryboat*, illustrated by Giulio. Use the words in the Word Bank to finish these sentences about the way a ferry runs.

1. To cross a river, you can go over a bridge or take a _____.
2. The ferry carries _____ and _____.
3. The _____ drives the ferry.
4. You can drive or _____ onto the ferry.
5. The _____ and back of the ferry are the same.
6. You need a _____ to ride the ferry.
7. _____ sometimes sprays your face.
8. The Captain watches for other _____.
9. The ferry slides into the narrow _____.
10. Cars and trucks drive over the _____.
11. If you miss a ferry, drive to a _____.
12. The ferry isn't used when _____ covers the river.

Word Bank						
boats	bridge	captain	cars	ferry	front	ice
ramp	slip	ticket	trucks	walk	water	

Name _____   Date _____

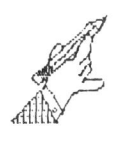

BRUCE COVILLE

Sarah's Unicorn; Sarah and the Dragon

Read *Sarah's Unicorn* and *Sarah's Dragon*. Sarah has so many magical adventures. You can create another one for her. Pick one of the following activities to do with these books.

1. Mag is saved by Oakhorn's magic horn. Think of a new problem for Mag in which Sarah, Oakhorn, and the animals save her.

Perhaps, Mag meets an evil witch, wizard, or gnome who tries to kidnap Sarah so Mag will give him or her a certain magic spell to turn toadstools into gold.

Maybe Sarah's other aunt wants to take her away from Mag.

Maybe Sarah's long-lost brother comes back from a sea voyage and wants Sarah to live with him.

2. Toad was placed under a spell. When he left his castle in the sky, he was a dragon. Write a story explaining why Toad was turned into a dragon. Who did it? Why did they do it? How was the spell to be broken? (That's in the story)

3. Now that Toad, Mag, Sarah, and Oakhorn are friends, write an adventure for them.

Maybe Mag and Toad will marry?

Maybe Toad's old enemy will bother Mag, Oakhorn, and Sarah because they helped Toad change back into himself.

Name _____ Date _____

ELOISE GREENFIELD

Honey, I Love

Read *Honey, I Love and Other Love Poems*. Read the poem "Harriet Tubman" again. Then read a biography of Harriet Tubman or read about her in an encyclopedia. The poem says she wasn't born to be a slave and she didn't stay that way. What did Harriet do about her situation? *Harriet Tubman, Conductor of the Underground Railroad* by Kate McMullan (Dial, 1991) is an excellent biography for grade 3.

Eloise had a wonderful idea for a biography book report. When she wrote "Harriet Tubman," she picked the essential idea, the most important idea, of Harriet's life and put it into a poem. Book reports don't need to be boring.

Pick a famous person you like.

Read a biography of that person or an article from an encyclopedia.

Write a poem about that person's most important trait.

Use the lines below to collect ideas for your poem from the biography you read.

_____

_____

_____

_____

_____

_____

_____

Name _____ **Date** _____

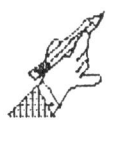

PHYLLIS HALLORAN

Cat Purrs

Read "My Cats" and "Wishing" from *Cat Purrs*. Phyllis must really love cats. She wrote so many poems about them. I think cats are nice, but I love monkeys. What animal do you love? Write several poems about the animal you love. They can be short just like the ones Phyllis wrote. Write your poems on the lines below. Share with a friend. Read the examples:

Monkey Laugh

Does my monkey laugh?
Of course—
When tickled by a giraffe!

Dreaming

Monkey's dreaming, I bet,
of a jungle deep, dark, and wet.
Or maybe a small treat,
sixty chocolate-covered bananas
to eat.

_____

_____

_____

_____

_____

Name _____   Date _____

PETER PARNALL

The Great Fish

Read *The Great Fish*. Use the words in the Word Bank to finish these sentences about a little boy listening to the legend his grandfather tells him.

1. Grandfather told the story of the salmon _____.

2. The salmon is the _____ of our people.

3. In the spring, _____ are nearly empty.

4. People grew _____.

5. There was much _____.

6. The mothers' _____ flowed to the _____.

7. The salmon swam to the _____ of the tears.

8. Schools of salmon _____ the river.

9. The braves _____ the salmon from the river with spears and _____.

10. They fished for three days and three _____.

11. The mothers stopped _____.

12. Every year the salmon _____.

Word Bank

| brother | crying | filled | hunger | nights | picked | return |
| river | source | spear | storerooms | tears | thin | traps |

Name _____   Date _____

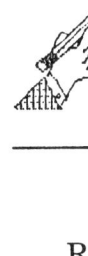

BROCK COLE

The Giant's Toe

Read *The Giant's Toe*. The poor giant isn't having any better of a time with this little toe/boy than he had with Jack. Except in the end, the toe/boy does the giant a gigantic favor.

1. The giant was hoeing his _____.

2. He hit his _____ and saw his _____.

3. He couldn't _____ or _____ it back on.

4. The giant planned to bake the toe in a _____.

5. Then he planned to throw him in a _____ to China.

6. Jack knocked at the _____.

7. He wanted the hen, and the _____.

8. Jack went looking for a different _____.

9. The toe and the giant _____ happily ever after.

10. The toe saved the giant's _____.

Word Bank

cabbages	foot	giant	gate	glue	harp
hole	life	lived	pie	sew	toe

Name _____   Date _____

MILLICENT SELSAM

Terry and the Caterpillars

Read *Terry and the Caterpillars*. Use the words in the Word Bank to finish these sentences about a little girl who watches a caterpillar become something beautiful!

1. Terry put her caterpillar in a _____.

2. It was _____ with orange and yellow bumps.

3. The caterpillar ate _____ tree leaves.

4. The caterpillar _____ itself in _____.

5. It made a _____.

6. A _____ crawled out.

7. It had _____ wings.

8. When the moth crawled out, it had _____ wings.

9. They grew as _____ traveled through them.

10. The mother moth leaves _____ on sticks.

11. They turn into _____.

12. And everything happens _____.

Word Bank							
again	apple	blood	brown	caterpillars	cocoon		
eggs	green	jar	moth	silk	small	wrapped	

Name _____ Date _____

ELAINE MOORE

<u>Mixed-Up Sam</u>

Read *Mixed-Up Sam*. Poor Sam is so confused. He does everything at the wrong time. Even his pets are confused. Fill in the lines below so Sam knows how to act.

Dear Sam,

We have noticed that something is wrong at your house. We'd like to help. Please think about this list of ideas.

1. Please eat breakfast in the _____.

2. Eat dinner at _____.

3. Cats should _____ and dogs should _____.

4. _____ when you're sad; _____ when you're happy.

5. A garden should grow in the _____.

6. Newspapers should be read from _____ to _____.

7. You read books; don't wear them as _____.

8. Do not bathe with _____ on.

Sincerely yours,

a friend _____
write your name here

Word Bank				
back	bark	clothes	cry	front
ground	hats	laugh	meow	morning	night

Name _____ Date _____

ELIZABETH COATSWORTH

The Cat Who Went to Heaven

NOTE TO THE TEACHER: Read *The Cat Who Went to Heaven*. This special story of Good Fortune the cat can lead to another investigation into the world of cats. Cats are a favorite animal. Throughout history, cats have been revered as very special and suspicious creatures. After you read the story, have the children study cats. Perhaps some have cats as pets. They can bring in pictures and talk about their pets.

Below are some questions children can consider when doing research on cats.

1. How old are cats?

2. What did the ancient Egyptians and others think about cats?

3. Are cats easy to care for?

4. What special needs do cats have?

5. If you have a cat, do a picture report about your cat entitled "A Week (or A Day) in the Life of My Cat" as an example for your students.

Use the lines below to write down other cat questions your students can research.

_____

_____

_____

_____

| ☆ Judy Delton |
| ☆ George Selden |
| ☆ Ellen McGregor |
| ☆ Oliver Butterworth |
| ☆ Edward Lear |
| ☆ Jay Williams |
| ☆ Mavis Jukes |
| ☆ Eloise Greenfield |
| ☆ May Intermediate |
| ☆ |

| ☆ Leo Lionni |
| ☆ Giulio Maestro |
| ☆ Lillian Hoban |
| ☆ Margaret Wise Brown |
| ☆ Martha Alexander |
| ☆ Millicent Selsam |
| ☆ Eloise Greenfield |
| ☆ Phyllis Halloran |
| ☆ May Primary II |
| ☆ |

| ☆ Don Wood |
| ☆ Judy Delton |
| ☆ Nonny Hogrogian |
| ☆ Carol Carrick |
| ☆ Arnold Lobel |
| ☆ Peter Parnall |
| ☆ Bruce Coville |
| ☆ Brock Cole |
| ☆ Elaine Moore |
| ☆ May Primary I |
| ☆ |

MAY ANSWER KEY

Mavis Jukes: *Like Jake and Me*

1. wood
2. twins
3. pears, bottle
4. ballet
5. wolf
6. Virginia
7. afraid
8. tooth
9. hat
10. danced, porch

Giulio Maestro: *Ferryboat*

1. ferry
2. cars, trucks
3. captain
4. walk
5. front
6. ticket
7. water
8. boats
9. slip
10. ramp
11. bridge
12. ice

Peter Parnall: *The Great Fish*

1. spear
2. brother
3. storerooms
4. thin
5. hunger
6. tears, river
7. source
8. filled
9. picked, traps
10. nights
11. crying
12. return

Brock Cole: *The Giant's Toe*

1. cabbages
2. foot, toe
3. glue, sew
4. pie
5. hole
6. gate
7. harp
8. giant
9. lived
10. life

Millicent Selsam: *Terry and the Caterpillars*

1. jar
2. green
3. apple
4. wrapped, silk
5. cocoon
6. moth
7. brown
8. small
9. blood
10. eggs
11. caterpillars
12. again

Elaine Moore: *Mixed-Up Sam*

1. morning
2. night
3. meow, bark
4. cry, laugh
5. ground
6. front, back
7. hats
8. clothes

MAY AUTHORS BIBLIOGRAPHY

May 3 Mavis Jukes

No One Is Going to Nashville (Knopf, 1983); *Like Jake and Me* (Knopf, 1984); *Lights Around the Palm* (Knopf, 1987)

May 6 Giulio Maestro

A Raft of Riddles (Dutton, 1982); *Halloween Howls: Riddles That Are a Scream* (Dutton, 1983); *Riddle Romp* (Houghton Mifflin, 1983); *What'a a Frank Frank? Tasty Homograph Riddles* (Clarion, 1984); *Razzle-Dazzle Riddles* (Clarion, 1985); *Ferryboat* by Betsy Maestro, illustrations by Giulio (Harper, 1986); *What's Mite Might? Homophone Riddles to Boost Your Word Power* (Clarion, 1986)

May 16 Bruce Coville

For primary children: *The Foolish Giant* (Harper, 1978); *Sarah's Unicorn* (Harper, 1979); *Sarah and the Dragon* (Harper, 1984); for third grade readers and up: *The Monster's Ring* (Pantheon, 1982); *Ghost in the Third Row* (Bantam, 1987); *Ghost Wore Gray* (Bantam, 1988); *How I Survived Summer Vacation* (Simon & Schuster, 1988); *Some of My Best Friends Are Monsters* (Simon & Schuster, 1988); *Monster of the Year* (Simon & Schuster, 1989); *My Teacher Is an Alien* (Simon & Schuster, 1989)

May 17 Eloise Greenfield

She Come Bringing Me That Little Baby Girl (Harper, 1974); *Me & Neesie* (Harper, 1975); *Grandmama's Joy* (Putnam, 1980); *Daydreamers* (Dial, 1981); *Honey, I Love & Other Love Poems* (Harper, 1986); *Grandpa's Face* (Putnam, 1988); *Under the Sunday Tree* (Harper, 1988); *Nathaniel Talking* (Writers & Readers, 1989)

May 21 Phyllis Halloran

Cat Purrs (Milliken, 1987); *Oh Brother! Oh Sister!* (Milliken, 1988); *Red Is My Favorite Color* (Reading, Inc., 1988); *I'd Like to Hear a Flower Grow* (Reading, Inc., 1989)

May 23 Peter Parnall

Hawk, I Am Your Brother by Byrd Baylor (Macmillan, 1976)—1977 Caldecott Honor Book; As author/illustrator: *The Mountain* (Doubleday, 1971); *The Great Fish* (Doubleday, 1973); *Alfalfa Hill* (Doubleday, 1975); *Winter Barn* (Macmillan, 1986); *Apple Tree* (Macmillan, 1988); *Feet* (Macmillan, 1988); *Cats From Away* (Macmillan, 1989); *Quiet* (Greenwillow, 1989); illustrator of the following: *Annie and the Old One* by Miska Miles (Little, Brown, 1971);

Everybody Needs a Rock by Byrd Baylor (Macmillan, 1974); *If You Are a Hunter of Fossils* by Byrd Baylor (Macmillan, 1980); *The Way to Start a Day* by Byrd Baylor (Macmillan, 1986)

May 29   Brock Cole

Winter Wren (Farrar, 1984); *The Giant's Toe* (Farrar, 1986)

May 30   Millicent Selsam

Easy-to-read nonfiction for grades 1-3: *Terry and the Caterpillars* (Harper, 1962); *Greg's Microscope* (Harper, 1963); *Hidden Animals* (Harper, 1969); *Sea Monsters of Long Ago* (Macmillan, 1978); *All About Eggs* (Harper, 1980); *Cotton* (Morrow, 1982); *Catnip* (Morrow, 1983); *Is This a Baby Dinosaur?* (Harper, 1984); *Where Do They Go? Insects in Winter* (Scholastic, 1984); *Egg to Chick* (Harper, 1987)

May 31   Elaine Moore

Grandma's House (Lothrop, 1985); *Grandma's Promise* (Lothrop, 1988); *Mixed-Up Sam* (Milliken, 1988)

May 31   Elizabeth Coatsworth

Third grade readers who like a challenge will enjoy these books: *The Cat Who Went to Heaven* (Macmillan, 1967)—1931 Newbery Award Book; *Daniel Webster's Horses* (Garrard, 1971); *Marra's World* (Greenwillow, 1975); *Under the Green Willow* (Greenwillow, 1984)

JUNE

June 5	Allan Ahlberg, *Funnybones* (writing activity)
June 6	Cynthia Rylant, *Night in the Country* (writing a sound book)
June 7	Gwendolyn Brooks, *Bronzeville Boys and Girls* (poetry)*
June 7	Judith Elkin, *A Family in Japan* (country research)*
June 10	Maurice Sendak, *Chicken Soup with Rice* (silly food menu)
June 11	Robert Munsch, *Love You Forever* (writing activity)
June 14	Bobbie Hamsa, *Your Pet Elephant* (writing activity)
June 14	Bruce Degen, *The Magic Schoolbus Inside the Human Body* (art activity)
June 17	Dorothy Haas, *New Friends* (making a book)
June 18	Pat Hutchins, *The Wind Blew* (writing activity)
June 24	Jean Marzollo, *The Best Present* (making predictions)
June 26	Lynd Ward, *The Biggest Bear* (word find)
June 27	Lucille Clifton, *The Boy Who Didn't Believe in Spring* (putting on a play)*

June Bookmarks
June Answer Key
June Authors Bibliography

*Denotes multicultural title/activity

JUNE AUTHORS

DATE	NAME	AUTHOR	ILLUSTRATOR	\multicolumn{4}{c}{READING LEVEL}			
				K	1	2	3
1	James Daugherty	X	X		X	X	X
2	Paul Galdone		X			X	X
3	Anita Lobel	X	X			X	X
5	Allan Ahlberg	X	X	X	X	X	X
5	Richard Scarry	X	X	X	X		
6	Verna Aardema	X		X	X	X	
6	Cynthia Rylant	X		X	X	X	X
6	Peter Spier	X	X	X	X	X	X
7	Gwendolyn Brooks	X				X	X
7	Judith Elkin	X				X	X
10	Maurice Sendak	X	X	X	X	X	X
11	Robert Munsch	X		X	X	X	X
14	Bruce Degen	X	X	X	X	X	X
14	Bobbie Hamsa	X				X	X
14	Janice May Udry	X		X	X	X	
17	Dorothy Haas	X				X	X
18	Pat Hutchins	X	X	X	X		
18	Chris Van Allsburg	X	X	X	X	X	X
21	Robert Kraus	X		X	X	X	
24	Jean Marzollo	X				X	X
25	Eric Carle	X	X	X	X	X	
26	Lynd Ward	X	X	X	X	X	X
26	Charlotte Zolotow	X		X	X	X	X
27	Lucille Clifton	X		X	X	X	X
30	David McPhail	X	X	X	X	X	

ALLAN AHLBERG

Funnybones

Read *Funnybones*. The skeletons work hard at scaring each other because everyone is asleep. But that is not true. Many people work at night. Do you know who they are? Read a book from your media center about night workers.

Write a story about the skeletons scaring some of these workers. Think about the following questions before you start your story. Use the lines below for ideas for your rough draft.

1. Who are the workers? How do the skeletons get to the place where these workers are?

2. How will they scare them?

3. What if the workers hit them and they fall apart? Who will put the skeletons back together?

_____

_____

_____

_____

_____

_____

Name _____ **Date** _____

CYNTHIA RYLANT

<u>Night in the Country</u>

Read *Night in the Country*. Night is special in the country and in the city. Day is also filled with special sounds. Write a story about special sounds. You can pick day or night sounds in the city or day or night sounds in the country. You can do day sounds at school, at home, or anywhere, any time. Use these questions to help you start.

1. Will you write about country, city, or school sounds, or something else?

_____

2. Will they be day or night sounds? _____

3. Make a list of all the sounds you have heard there at that time. Use a blank piece of paper.

4. Decide on the important sounds.

5. Write a story to explain those sounds to someone younger than you. Use words that describe those sounds.

Here's the beginning of my story:

There is no day so noisy as the last day of school.

In room after room, you can hear, "Children, please! We only have thirty minutes to wait."

Lockers clang and bang. Children scuffle and shuffle their desks to the wall. They play games, shouting each rule.

There are teacher sighing. Mothers crying, "Is it really the last day of school already?"

Children dream of sleeping late, going to their swimming pool. They dream about getting cool. . .

GET BUSY WITH YOUR SOUND STORY!

Name _____   Date _____

GWENDOLYN BROOKS

Bronzeville Boys and Girls

NOTE TO THE TEACHER: Read *Bronzeville Boys and Girls* to your children. There are a number of activities to do with this book. Here are three.

1. Gertrude loves to hear Marian Anderson sing. Check out a Marian Anderson record from the media center. Have the children write a poem as they listen to her sing.

2. Have the children write a poem about themselves. Put all the poems in a classbook. Title the book, _____ *Boys and Girls* (fill in the blank with the name of your town).

3. Ask the children if they would like to write a poem about one of the topics Gwendolyn used. Compare their poem to the one Gwendolyn wrote. TOPICS:

Tea party; when parents chase you out of the house; when relatives visit; imagination at play; dreams of parents; secret places; being sad; snow; less fortunate people; being good in party clothes; living in an apartment; a secret treasure; babysitting a brother or sister; fear of thunder and lightning; people who are rich; going to church or services; death of a pet; a tree; stars; a pet cat or other animal; a night with the family; love of parents.

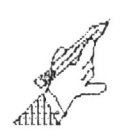

JUDITH ELKIN

A Family in Japan

NOTE TO THE TEACHER: You and your children can be jetsetters, traveling to all corners of the world with a series of *A Family In...* books.

As an adjunct study to family life, this Lerner series takes an in-depth look at family life in various countries. Topics discussed are; hometown in relation to big cities, home life, school life and expectations, religious holidays, sports, and many more.

Show the children a small map of the world. Tell them they will draw a large wall-map size projection of all the continents with major countries. Have the children select a country to study. The countries in the Lerner series are: Australia, Bolivia, Brazil, Chile, China, Egypt, France, India, Ireland, Italy, Jamaica, Japan, Liberia, Morocco, Nigeria, Pakistan, Peru, Singapore, Sri Lanka, and West Germany. Other titles include: An Aboriginal, Arab, and Eskimo family.

With these materials and a set of reading goals, students can learn what life is like outside their own small neighborhoods.

Establish goals for the reports. Here are some to think about.

1. Children can compare living quarters to their own.

2. Children can compare style of schooling to their own.

3. Children can compare eating habits to their own.

4. Children can compare religious beliefs to their own.

5. Children can compare climate of another country to their own.

6. Children can compare style of dress to their own.

7. Children can compare games and forms of entertainment to their own.

Through all this, they will learn the reasons for differences and understand that being different is what makes each country and person uniquely wonderful.

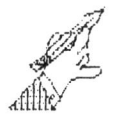

MAURICE SENDAK

Chicken Soup With Rice

Read *Chicken Soup With Rice*. That really is one of my favorite soups. But I really like ice cream better.

Have you ever been to one of those ice cream places that serves 566 flavors? Let's see which of those is your favorite. Put an X on your answer.

Would you rather eat:

____ Pickled Marshmallow Fudge

        or

____ Carmel Mustard Ripple

____ Pork and Bean Delight or ____ Peanut Kraut Surprise

____ Coffee Corn Almond Chocolate

        or

____ Cheddar Apple Crunch Dream

Make up six tasty treats of your own. Ask a friend to pick the ones he or she likes best!

1. _____
2. _____
3. _____
4. _____
5. _____
6. _____

Name _____ Date _____

ROBERT MUNSCH
Love You Forever

    Read *Love You Forever.* As the little boy grows into a man, he keeps hearing that one phrase in his mother's song. Does your mother or father have a special phrase besides "I Love You"? Use the lines below to collect different phases your mom or dad use. Use one to write a song and create a story as Robert did.

_____

_____

_____

_____

_____

_____

_____

Name _____ **Date** _____

BOBBIE HAMSA

Your Pet Elephant

Read *Your Pet Elephant*. Bobbie wrote a special story that is a mixture of real and unreal ideas. People don't really keep elephants in their homes. But elephants really do need certain things when they are kept in a zoo.

Pick an animal that you really wouldn't be able to have as a pet. Use an encyclopedia or book to discover information about the following ideas. When you have answered the questions, write a story about your pretend pet the way Bobbie Hamsa did.

1. Where does your pet come from? _____
_____

2. What does it need for care and feeding? _____
_____
_____

3. How big will it get? _____

4. How much will it eat as an adult? _____

5. Does it need special sleeping arrangements? _____

What: _____
_____

6. In what ways will it need to be trained? _____
_____
_____

Good luck with your story!

Name _____   Date _____

BRUCE DEGEN

The Magic Schoolbus Inside the Human Body

NOTE TO THE TEACHER: Read *The Magic Schoolbus Inside the Human Body*. Explain to the children that Bruce not only writes and illustrates his own books, but he also illustrates the work of others. This book is filled with great pieces of information about the human body. You can see the reports written by the children throughout the entire book. They are short and to the point.

My favorite part of the book is toward the end, when all the children are working on a huge chart of the human body. You can do that with your children, too.

Take some mural, butcher, or bulletin board paper. Trace a human body with all its parts. Color and label it. Have the children write small reports about different body parts, and hang the reports on the wall around the body chart.

DOROTHY HAAS

Peanut Butter and Jelly Series : New Friends

NOTE TO THE TEACHER:

Dorothy Haas' series about Peanut and Jilly is excellent reading material for reluctant readers or those reading at a third grade level. The stories are full of real emotions and life situations.

To use the Dorothy Haas booklet, simply fold it like a greeting card, in half and in half again. Now the children can check off the titles as they read them.

A blank format for "Books I Love" follows Dorothy's booklet. Children can write the names of the books they read on the inside. They can also create their own series booklet for an author they like to read. They can decorate the cover, too! Other examples for author booklets might include: Patricia Reilly Giff, James Marshall, Byrd Baylor, Don and Audrey Wood, Steven Kellogg—or anyone the children or you select. Have fun with the blank booklet and with reading a series.

Other Peanut Butter and Jelly titles
by Dorothy Haas.

Place an X in front of the titles you
have read.

___ New Friends

___ The Haunted House

___ Peanut and Jilly Forever

___ Not Starring Jilly

___ Peanut in Charge

___ Trouble at Alcott School

___ Alcott Library is Falling Down

BOOKS BY
DOROTHY
HAAS
I
HAVE
READ

HERE ARE MY FAVORITES:

_____
_____
_____
_____
_____

I LOVE BOOKS

WRITTEN BY

_____

PAT HUTCHINS

The Wind Blew

Read *The Wind Blew*. The wind is such a nasty wind. I'm sure it won't be nice once it blows out to sea. What kinds of ships and boats will it bother on the sea? Look for books about ships and boats in the media center.

Write a story about the *Nasty Wind Over the Sea*. Use the lines below to write the names of the boats the wind will bother.

_____

_____

_____

_____

_____

_____

_____

_____

Name _____ **Date** _____

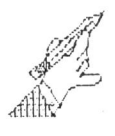

JEAN MARZOLLO

39 Kids on the Block: The Best Present Ever

Good readers listen to themselves when they read. They hear the story as well as see it with their eyes. A good reader makes predictions. If you are really into a story, you can usually guess what happens next. Read Chapter 1 of *The Best Present Ever*. Write several events that you think will happen next.

Here are my predictions for Chapter 2. Write your predictions below. Read Chapter 2 to see if we are right.

Make predictions whenever you feel you know what is going to happen. A prediction sheet follows this one. Have fun making predictions. They will make you a better reader!

Rusty could get an Amazon Indian mask for Christmas from his parents.

Grandma could go to church with him on Christmas— that would be a special present.

They could put a very small Christmas tree in the living room.

So many things could happen. What are your predictions? Read the rest of the story to see if you are good at predicting.

_____

_____

_____

_____

_____

Name _____ Date _____

Prediction Sheet

Title _____

_____

_____

_____

_____

_____

_____

_____

_____

_____

_____

Name _____ **Date** _____

LYND WARD

The Biggest Bear

Read *The Biggest Bear.* Find the words from the Word Bank in the word search puzzle below.

```
F W V G S R T O U J H B S B U M S
V M F P G E S R V N T A C E N Z S
H B Y G C D V W X Z V M M X G T U
Q Q J Z O L X N W F R V I S I T T
R Y I O N S G A W N H H E U M F U
W S W O H C U B J M H K H G K K X
T M C O R N O R V M A F M A P L E
B A P D P C N R S C U S J R U B Q
B Q X K U B H Y N Y W A H R Y V C
I Y P A T B E A R S K I N Q K K I
S H K J F L P P R H I Q R M T F O
N A M T L I L P D D B K U B B H J
C S F A V G M L R Z U V L X F Z Y
L I V Z T H I E X Y V K I A D F J
G Z T I M W L S T M W B U R E X T
Y N X D P B K I G Z O Z F C V M L
```

Word Bank

apples	bacon	bearskin	corn	cub	hams
Johnny	maple	mash	milk	orchard	pancakes
sugar	valley	visit	wild	woods	zoo

Name _____ Date _____

LUCILLE CLIFTON

The Boy Who Didn't Believe in Spring

NOTE TO THE TEACHER: You and your children can be stage designers, actors, prop crew, and playwrights. Have children rewrite *The Boy Who Didn't Believe in Spring* in their own words.

A mural of buildings can serve as a proper backdrop to the play.

The cast of characters would be King Shabazz, Tony, Mama, Teacher, and brother Sam.

Children can be creative and actually create dialogue to show what the Mom and Teacher could have said at home and at school.

The narrator's part can rotate to all children, as there are large segments of text in which the main characters do not have dialogue.

All children can be prop hands by bringing the concrete objects shown in the pictures.

All these activities bring literature alive for children. They will see that stories are not just fiction. They are little snippets of true-life experiences that other people have lived and that other children are living. The real story goes on even as they pretend.

Primary I

- Robert Munsch
- Bobbie Hamsa
- Anita Lobel
- Cynthia Rylant
- Maurice Sendak
- Chris Van Allsburg
- Allan Ahlberg
- Bruce Degen
- Lynd Ward
- Beatrice Schenk DeRegniers

June
Primary I

Primary II

- Paul Galdone
- Peter Spier
- Pat Hutchins
- Robert Kraus
- Charlotte Zolotow
- Nancy Willard
- Lucille Clifton
- Gwendolyn Brooks
- Richard Scarry
- Verna Aardema

June
Primary II

Intermediate

- Cynthia Rylant
- Linda Glovach
- Elizabeth Orton Jones
- Robert Burch
- Dorothy Haas
- Judith Elkin
- Gwendolyn Brooks
- John Ciardi
- Antoine de Saint Exupery

June
Intermediate

JUNE ANSWER KEY

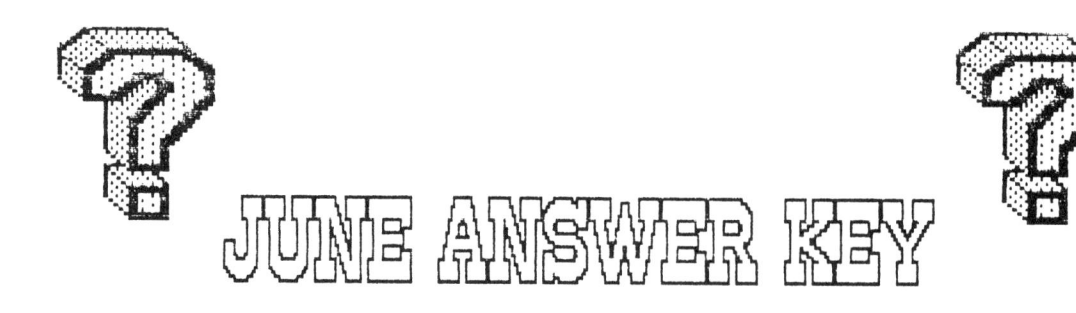

Lynd Ward: *The Biggest Bear*

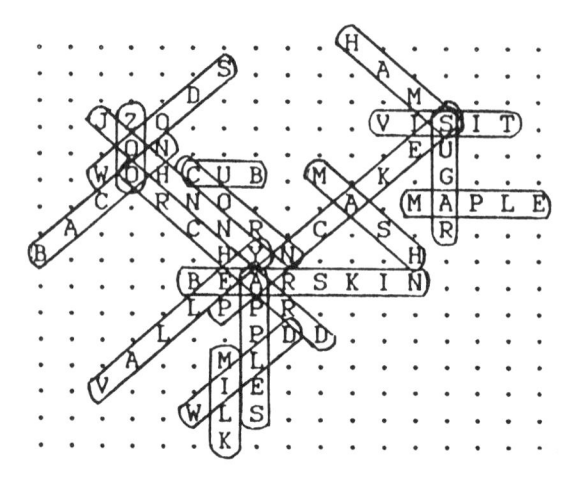

JUNE AUTHORS BIBLIOGRAPHY

June 5 Allan Ahlberg
Funnybones (Greenwillow, 1981); all published by Viking Penguin: *Woof!* (1986); *The Cinderella Show* (1987); *The Clothes Horse and Other Stories* (1988); *The Mighty Slide* (1988); *Starting School* (1988); *Ten in a Bed* (1989)

June 6 Cynthia Rylant
When I Was Young in the Mountains (Dutton, 1982)—1983 Caldecott Award Book; *This Year's Garden* (Bradbury, 1984); *The Relatives Came* (Bradbury, 1985); *Night in the Country* (Bradbury, 1986); *Birthday Presents* (Orchard, 1987); *Henry & Mudge* series published by Bradbury, 1987

June 7 Gwendolyn Brooks
Bronzeville Boys and Girls (Harper, 1956); *Selected Poems* (Harper, 1963)

June 7 Judith Elkin
A Family in Japan (Lerner, 1987)

June 10 Maurice Sendak
Wonderful selection of titles for preschool through third grade: illustrated *What Do You Say, Dear* by Sesyle Joslin (Scholastic, 1980)—1959 Caldecott Honor Book; *Alligators All Around* (Harper, 1962); *Chicken Soup with Rice* (Harper, 1962); *One Was Johnny* (Harper, 1962); *Outside Over There* (Harper, 1962); *Pierre* (Harper, 1962); *Where The Wild Things Are* (Harper, 1963)—1964 Caldecott Award Book; *In the Night Kitchen* (Harper, 1970); *Some Swell Pup* (Farrar, 1976); *Seven Little Monsters* (Harper, 1977)

June 11 Robert Munsch
All titles available in rebound paperback from Story House Corporation, Bindery Lane, Charlotteville, NY 12036: *Paper Bag Princess* (1980); *Mud Puddle* (1982); *David's Father* (1983); *Millicent and the Wind* (1984); *Thomas' Snowsuit* (1985); *Boy in the Drawer* (1986); *Love You Forever* (1986). He has more titles, but these are my favorites!

June 14 Bobbie Hamsa
All published by Children's Press: *Your Pet Elephant* (1980); *Your Pet Gorilla* (1981); *Your Pet Lion* (1981); *Your Pet Bear* (out of print); *Your Pet Beaver* (out of print); *Your Pet Camel* (out of print); *Your Pet Giraffe* (out of print)

June 14 Bruce Degen

His own titles include: *Aunt Possum and the Pumpkin Man* (Harper, 1977); *Little Witch and the Riddle* (Harper, 1980); *Jamberry* (Harper, 1983); the illustrator of other books: *Commander Toad* series by Jane Yolen; *Magic Schoolbus* series by Joanna Cole; *Dandelion Hill* by Clyde Robert Bulla (January 9 author) (Dutton, 1982)

June 17 Dorothy Haas

Peanut Butter and Jelly series published by Scholastic: *The Haunted House* (1988); *New Friends* (1988); *Peanut and Jilly Forever* (1988); *Not Starring Jilly!* (1989); *Peanut in Charge* (1989); *Trouble at Alcott School* (1989); *Poppy and the Outdoors Cat* (Whitman, 1982); *The Secret Life of Dilly McBean* (Bradbury, 1986)

June 18 Pat Hutchins

Published by Greenwillow for grades 3-5: *Curse of the Egyptian Mummy* (1983); published by Macmillan: *Rosie's Walk* (1971); *Titch* (1971); *The Wind Blew* (1974); *Surprise Party* (1986); *Changes, Changes* (1987); *Good Night Owl* (1987); Read-Alone books published by Greenwillow: *Don't Forget the Bacon!* (1976); *Happy Birthday Sam* (1978); *Tale of Thomas Mead* (1980); *One Hunter* (1982); *You'll Soon Grow Into Them, Titch* (1983); *Very Worst Monster* (1985); *The Doorbell Rang* (1986)

June 24 Jean Marzollo

39 Kids on the Block series, perfect for second graders, published by Scholastic (1989-1990): *Best Friends Club; The Best Present Ever; Chicken Pox Strikes; The Green Ghost of Appleville, Roses Are Pink and You Stink; Uproar of Hollercat Hill* (Dial, 1980); *Jed and the Space Bandits* (Dial, 1987); *Soccer Sam* (Random, 1987); *Silver Bear* (Dial, 1987); *Red-Ribbon Rosie* (Random, 1988); *Pizza Pie Slugger* (Random, 1989); *Teddy Bear Book* (Dial, 1989)

June 26 Lynd Ward

The Biggest Bear (Houghton Mifflin, 1952)—1953 Caldecott Award Book; *Silver Pony: A Story in Pictures* (Houghton Mifflin, 1973)

June 27 Lucille Clifton

The Boy Who Didn't Believe in Spring (Dutton, 1973); *Everett Anderson* series published by Holt (1988): *Everett Anderson's Goodbye; Everett Anderson's Nine Month Long; Some of the Days of Everett Anderson*

JULY

July 4	Stephen Mooser, *My Hollywood Boyfriend* (booklet)
July 10	Fred Gwynne, *A Chocolate Moose for Dinner* (art activity)
July 11	James Stevenson, *Emma* (writing activity)
July 13	Marcia Brown, *Shadow* (shadow mask making)*
July 14	Laura Joffe Numeroff, *If You Give a Mouse a Cookie* (writing activity)
July 16	Arnold Adoff, *In for Winter, Out for Spring* (poem)*
July 16	Ida De Lage, *The Farmer and the Witch* (fill in)
July 24	Amy Ehrlich, *Bunnies All Day Long* (writing activity)
July 24	Charlotte Pomerantz, *The Chalk Doll* (doll making)*
July 25	Ron Barrett, *Animals Should Definitely Not Act Like People* (writing activity)
July 26	Stephen Cosgrove, *Shimmeree* (writing activity)
July 28	Natalie Babbitt, *The Devil's Storybook* (word search)

July Bookmarks
July Answer Key
July Authors Bibliography

*Denotes multicultural title/activity

JULY AUTHORS

DATE	NAME	AUTHOR/ILLUSTRATOR	READING LEVEL			
			K	1	2	3
2	Jack Gantos	X			X	X
4	Stephen Mooser	X				X
10	Fred Gwynne	X	X	X	X	X	X
10	Martin Provensen	X	X	X	X	X	X
11	E. B. White	X					X
11	James Stevenson	X	X	X	X	X	
13	Marcia Brown	X		X	X		
14	Laura Numeroff	X		X	X	X	
14	Peggy Parish	X		X	X	X	
15	Clement Moore	X		X	X	X	
16	Arnold Adoff	X		X	X	X	X
16	Ida De Lage	X		X	X	X	X
16	Richard Egielski		X	X	X	X	
23	Patricia Coombs	X		X	X	X	
23	Robert Quackenbush	X	X			X	X
24	Amy Ehrlich	X		X	X	X	
24	Charlotte Pomerantz	X		X	X	X	
25	Ron Barrett	X	X	X	X	X	
26	Jan Berenstain	X		X	X	X	
26	Stephen Cosgrove	X		X	X	X	
27	Scott Corbett	X					X
28	Natalie Babbitt	X		X	X	X	X
28	Beatrix Potter	X	X	X	X	X	X

STEPHEN MOOSER

My Halloween Boyfriend

NOTE TO THE TEACHER:

To use the Stephen Mooser booklet on the following page, simply fold it like a greeting card, in half and in half again. Now the children can check off the titles as they read them.

This series is excellent for middle-of-the-year second graders and reluctant third graders. As we will always have at least a small percentage of reluctant readers, it's wonderful to have quality authors like Stephen who offer children good stories at a level they can handle.

Other Creature Club titles
by Stephen Mooser

Place and X in front of the titles you have read.

___ My Halloween Boyfriend

___ Monsters in the Outfield

___ Monster Holiday

___ The Fright-Face Contest

___ That's So Funny, I Forgot to Laugh

___ Crazy Mixed-Up Valentines

STEPHEN MOOSER

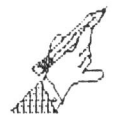

FRED GWYNNE
A Chocolate Moose for Dinner

Read *A Chocolate Moose for Dinner* or *A Little Pigeon Toad* or *The King Who Rained,* or all three! Homophones are words that sound the same but have different meanings and usually different spellings. Homographs are words that are spelled the same, but have entirely different meanings. Fred did a great job of showing the little boy's confusion over both of these kinds of words.

Draw pictures to go with several of these homophone problems. Collect your own homophones and illustrate them.

"Send in the picture," said the coach.

"Did you see the mountain peek?" asked the climber.

"Does your computer have 128K?" asked the salesman.

"Do you like locks and bagels?" asked the waitress.

"The first baseman swings a mean bat," said the reporter.

"I'm tired of bills in the mail," said mommy.

"Don't be a loafer," said the father to his lazy son.

"You look pail," said my mother.

"Why did the silly boy pick up the phone when he bumped his foot?"

    He was calling a toe (tow) truck.

"Why was the queen angry at the maids?"

    They couldn't keep the prince (prints) off the furniture.

Place one saying on a clean piece of paper and draw a *pitcher* to go with it. Have fun!!

For a rather extensive listing of homophones and homographs, check *The New Reading Teacher's Book of Lists* by Edward Fry et al (Prentice-Hall, 1985).

Name _____ Date _____

JAMES STEVENSON

Emma

Read *Emma*. Can you believe that Dolores and Lavinia? They are rotten to the core. I love the nice, but tricky way Emma gets back at those ugly old witches. That was a good story, but I know a better one. It's the one you're going to write. Remember the time Dolores and Lavinia wanted to win the "Wicked Witch" Trophy for the nastiest potion? They wanted to try it out on Emma. Roland overheard them and warned Emma. How did Emma get out of that pickle?

Write a story about *The Wicked Witch Trophy*. Use the lines below to collect ideas for your rough draft.

_____

_____

_____

_____

_____

_____

Name _____ Date _____

MARCIA BROWN
Shadow

Read *Shadow*. This Caldecott Award winning book is filled with the most beautiful pictures of shadows, shapes, and color. One of the pictures is a mask of "Shadow" itself. Marcia Brown used her imagination to bring shape and color to "Shadow."

Use the space below to draw your version of "Shadow." Think about colors, shape, designs, eyes, nose, and mouth. Be a creative Caldecott artist. If everyone in your class does this activity, you will have a book of masks. Redraw and paint your mask on heavy brown paper. Save it for Halloween.

Name _____   Date _____

LAURA JOFFE NUMEROFF

If You Give a Mouse a Cookie

Read *If You Give a Mouse a Cookie*. What a mess— the never-ending adventure! This story is a circle story. The events of the story lead right back to the beginning of the story. We can write circle stories, too.

Pick one of these story ideas and write a circle story of your own. Draw the pictures for it or work with an illustrator who is in your room. Or create your own title.

Use the lines below to start ideas for your rough draft.

If You Give a Horse a Carrot.

If You Give a Hamster a Tomato.

If You Give a Dog a Bone.

If You Give a Cat a Ball of Yarn.

If You Give a Bat a Peach.

If You Give Your Brother a Dollar.

If You Give Your Mom a Headache.

_____

_____

_____

_____

_____

Name _____ **Date** _____

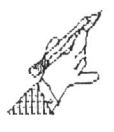

ARNOLD ADOFF

In for Winter, Out for Spring

Read *In for Winter, Out for Spring*. Becky tells us about many things: herself, her home, the first snow, a mouse in the house, a song to encourage spring, moving plants, finding a dog, and many others.

Find a poem that you like by Arnold. Write a poem on the same topic. Experiment with the way you place your lines. Do you see why Arnold changes the spacing of his lines from the way others do it? It is different but not just different. The spacing changes the way you read the poem and lets the reader see important ideas easily.

Use the lines below to write ideas for the rough draft of your poem. Illustrate your poem on a new piece of paper. If everyone in your class does this activity, you can create a class book of poems.

_____

_____

_____

_____

_____

_____

_____

_____

Name _____   Date _____

IDA DELAGE

The Farmer and the Witch

Read *The Farmer and the Witch*. Use the words in the Word Bank to finish the sentences about a tricky witch and a smart farmer.

1. A farmer looked for his bull, but found a _____.
2. She tried to _____ the farmer.
3. A _____ stuck to her foot.
4. The farmer's wife changed it into a _____.
5. The witch made a magic _____, but crashed into the _____.
6. Everything in the barnyard was _____.
7. The farmer and his wife made all the animals walk _____.
8. The witch's most _____ potion went into the well.
9. The farmer's wife said a pink-eyed hoppy _____ would help.
10. The farmer went to bed and _____.

Word Bank

backwards	confused	pie	potion	powerful	
pumpkin	scare	silo	snored	toad	witch

Name _____ Date _____

AMY EHRLICH

Bunnies All Day Long

Read *Bunnies All Day Long*. Harry, Larry and Paulette had a very busy day. But this story is about a school day. What problems do you think the rabbit children would cause on a Saturday morning?

Use the lines below to write ideas for a rough draft about "Saturday With the Bunnie Family." Write your story on a clean piece of paper.

Name _____ Date _____

CHARLOTTE POMERANTZ

The Chalk Doll

Read *The Chalk Doll*. Rose and her mother have a wonderful story time. The true stories of a mother's youth let us see our mothers as we never will, as children. Talk to your mother and father about dolls they might have had when they were young. My mother finally made me toss out my old teddy bear when I was fourteen. I often still miss it. It was made of smooth, shiny black felt with a blue and white set of overalls, blue thread eyes, and a red thread nose.

Ask your parents to help you make a rag doll, a teddy bear, or other doll from their youth. Write the story of how they first received their dolls. Share with friends in your class. Use the lines below to write ideas for your rough draft.

Name _____ Date _____

RON BARRETT

Animals Should Definitely Not Act Like People

Read *Animals Should Definitely Not Act Like People*. Ron and Judi have several good ideas here. But they didn't finish the sentences. They wanted you to do it for them. Start with the picture of the panda. It would be preposterous for a panda to *take a panda bear to bed*.

Use the lines below to finish six other sentences in the story. The first one is started for you.

because a worm would be worn out if he lifted weights or
if he tried to be a weightlifter or
if he wanted to be a bodybuilder

_____

_____

_____

_____

_____

_____

Name _____   Date _____

STEPHEN COSGROVE

Shimmeree

Read *Shimmeree*. Stephen's story is a good example of how people react to new things, people, or ideas. Pretend you are like Shimmeree. If you found a seed, what would it look like? What would come out of it?

Use the lines below to write ideas for your rough draft of "The Secret Seed," a story of a lovely new thing.

_____

_____

_____

_____

_____

_____

_____

_____

Name _____ Date _____

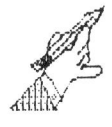

NATALIE BABBITT

The Devil's Storybook

Read "Wishes" from *The Devil's Storybook*. Find the words from the Word Bank in the word search puzzle below.

```
B S Q O B D W V V I U X Z O L
L O K R O I E R R L J M U Z W
K U T X Y S Z U Q W H F Y N Z
J L K H A O R H S I Z A J T D
D R C U E P U A Q F A R M X F
K I N G P R I N C E J E G I X
R B W C P U F D G S F V R G I
Q D F A A T C S I T R Y Z G N
L N H C G A H O Q O A R Z X N
T T V I C T I M N F K J Q I K
C T B T L C Z E T T H M A N H
O G B A S O F M R D E V I L O
S Z E H O X S E Y K L N S D D
S H E D K N O H O V L H T E V
W P Y E N P M M X N Z M Y E C
K N N K B D S T H D N E Z Q D
```

Word Bank

bother	boy	contented	devil	farm	handsome
health	hell	king	man	prince	rich
smoke	soul	vain	victim	wife	young

Name _____ Date _____

Jack Gantos	Ron Barrett	E. B. White
Marcia Brown	Peggy Parish	Natalie Babbitt
Amy Ehrlich	Stephen Cosgrove	Scott Corbett
Margery Williams	Eve Merriam	Eve Titus
Robert Quackenbush	Patricia Coombs	Stephen Mooser
Beatrix Potter	Jan Berenstain	Margery Williams
Fred Gwynne	Ida DeLage	Beatrix Potter
Laura Joffe Numeroff	Arnold Adoff	
Charlotte Pomerantz	Martin Provensen	Julian May writes as Ian Thorne

July
Primary I

July
Primary II

July
Intermediate

JULY ANSWER KEY

Ida DeLage: *The Farmer and the Witch*

1. witch
2. scare
3. pumpkin
4. pie
5. potion, silo
6. confused
7. backwards
8. powerful
9. toad
10. snored

Natalie Babbitt: *The Devil's Storybook*

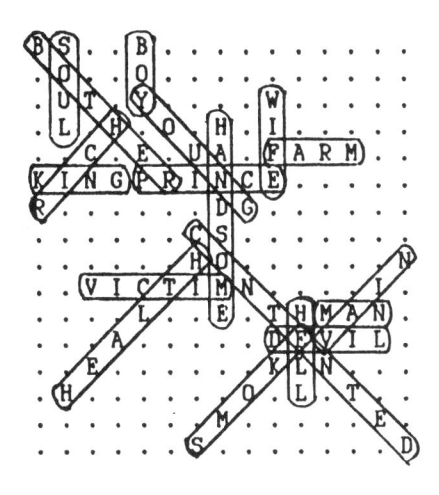

JULY AUTHORS BIBLIOGRAPHY

July 4   Stephen Mooser

The *Creepy Creatures Club* series published by Dell (1989-1990); *Crazy Mixed-Up Valentines; The Fright-Face Contest; Monster Holiday; Monster of the Year; Monsters in the Outfield; My Halloween Boyfriend; Night of the Vampire Kitty; Secrets of Scary Fun; That's So Funny, I Forgot to Laugh; Monster Express* (Archway, 1986); *Case of the Slippery Sharks* (Troll, 1987); *Funnyman Meets the Monster from Outer Space* (Scholastic, 1987)

July 10   Fred Gwynne

All published by Simon & Schuster/Prentice Hall: *The Sixteen-Hand Horse* (1987); *A Chocolate Moose for Dinner* (1988); *The King Who Rained* (1988); *A Little Pigeon Toad* (1990)

July 11   James Stevenson

The *Emma* series published by Greenwillow: *Yuck!* (1984); *Emma* (1985); *Happy Valentine's Day, Emma!* (1987); *Emma at the Beach* (1990); other titles published by Greenwillow: *Fast Friends* (1979); *The Night After Christmas* (1981); *Fried Feathers for Thanksgiving* (1986); *That Terrible Halloween Night* (1990)

July 13   Marcia Brown

(a multi Caldecott winner!) All published by Macmillan: *Stone Soup* (1947)—1948 Caldecott Honor Book; *Cinderella* (1981, paperback)—1955 Caldecott Award Book; *Once a Mouse* (1982, paperback)—1962 Caldecott Award Book; *Shadow* (1986, paperback)—1983 Caldecott Award Book

July 14   Laura Joffe Numeroff

Digger (Dutton, 1983); *If You Give a Mouse a Cookie* (Harper, 1985); *If You Give a Moose a Muffin* (Harper, 1991)

July 16   Arnold Adoff

Black Is Brown Is Tan (Harper, 1973); *Eats: Poems* (Lothrop, 1979); *Friend Dog* (Harper, 1980); *Birds* (Harper, 1982); *The Cabbages Are Chasing the Rabbits* (HBJ, 1985); *Greens* (Lothrop, 1988); *Chocolate Dreams* (Lothrop, 1989); *In for Winter, Out for Spring* (HBJ, 1991)

July 16   Ida De Lage

All published by Garrard: *The Farmer and the Witch* (1966); the *Old Witch* series: *Old Witch Goes to the Ball* (1969); *Old Witch and the Snores* (1970); *Old Witch and the Wizard* (1974); *Old Witch's Party* (1976); *Old Witch and the Ghost Parade* (1978); *Old Witch and Her Magic Basket* (1978); *Old Witch and the Dragon* (1979); *Old Witch Finds a New House* (1979); *Old Witch Gets a*

Surprise (1981); *Old Witch and the Crows* (1983). NOTE: Chelsea House is reprinting many of the *Old Witch* titles, so check your library or bookstore.

July 24 Amy Ehrlich

All published by Dial Books: *Leo, Zack and Emmie* (1981); *Bunnies and Their Grandma* (1985); *Bunnies at Christmastime* (1986); *Bunnies on Their Own* (1986); *Leo, Zack and Emmie Together Again* (1987); *Bunnies All Day Long* (1989); *Rapunzel* (1989)

July 24 Charlotte Pomerantz

Posy (Greenwillow, 1983); *The Tamarindo Puppy and Other Poems* (Greenwillow, 1980); *Where's the Bear?* (Greenwillow, 1984); *Whiff, Sniff, Nibble and Chew: The Gingerbread Boy Retold* (Greenwillow, 1984); *Timothy Tall Feather* (Greenwillow, 1986); *The Chalk Doll* (Lippincott, 1989)

July 25 Ron Barrett

With Judi Barrett: *Animals Should Definitely Not Wear Clothing* (Atheneum, 1970); *Benjamin's 365 Birthdays* (Macmillan, 1978); *Cloudy with a Chance of Meatballs* (Macmillan, 1978); *Animals Should Definitely Not Act Like People* (Atheneum, 1980); *A Snake Is Totally Tall* (Macmillan, 1983); *What's Left?* (Macmillan, 1983); *Pickles Have Pimples and Other Silly Statements* (Macmillan, 1986)

July 26 Stephen Cosgrove

Over 35 modern-day fairy tales with an assortment of real and unreal animals published by Price, Stern, including: *Bangalee; Buttermilk; Leo the Lop;* and *Shimmeree*

July 28 Natalie Babbitt

For primary: *The Something* (Farrarr, 1970); for grades 2-3: *The Devil's Storybook* (Farrar, 1974); *The Devil's Other Storybook* (Farrar, 1987)

AUGUST

August 3	Mary Calhoun, *Jack and the Whoopie Wind* (word meaning)
August 4	Nancy White Carlstrom, *Better Not Get Wet, Jesse Bear* (fill in)
August 6	Barbara Cooney, *Island Boy* (family tree)
August 9	Patricia McKissack, *Mirandy and Brother Wind* (writing activity)*
August 9	Jose Aruego (and Ariane Dewey Aruego, August 17), *How the Sun Was Brought Back to the Sky* (fill in)
August 11	Don Freeman, *Corduroy* and *A Pocket for Corduroy* (writing activity)*
August 11	Joanna Cole, *Bony Legs* (fill in)*
August 12	Audrey Wood, *Heckedy Peg* (writing activity)
August 21	X. J. Kennedy, *Brats* (poems)
August 26	Bernard Wiseman, *Morris Tells Boris Mother Moose Stories and Rhymes* (story starter)
August 27	Graham Oakley, *The Church Mice at Bay* (English word meanings)
August 28	Beau Gardner, *The Look Again . . . and Again, and Again, and Again Book* (art activity)

August Bookmarks
August Answer Key
August Authors Bibliography

*Denotes multicultural title/activity

AUGUST AUTHORS

DATE	NAME	AUTHOR/ILLUSTRATOR		K	1	2	3
2	James Howe	X		X	X	X	X
3	Mary Calhoun	X			X	X	
4	Nancy White Carlstrom	X	X	X	X		
6	Barbara Cooney	X	X	X	X	X	
6	Frank Asch	X	X	X	X		
7	Betsy Byars	X			X	X	
8	Trinka Hakes Noble	X		X	X	X	
8	Jan Plenkowski	X	X	X	X		
9	Patricia McKissack	X		X	X	X	X
9	Jose Aruego		X				
11	Don Freeman	X	X	X	X	X	
11	Steven Kroll	X		X	X	X	
11	Joanna Cole	X		X	X	X	
11	Jane Thayer	X		X	X	X	
12	Audrey Wood	X	X	X	X	X	
14	Robert Crowe	X		X	X	X	
14	Alice Provensen	X	X	X	X	X	X
15	Mark Taylor	X		X	X	X	
15	Brinton Turkle	X	X	X	X	X	
16	Matt Christopher	X					X
17	Ariane Dewey (Aruego)		X	X	X	X	
18	Louise Fatio	X		X	X	X	
21	X. J. Kennedy	X				X	X
21	Arthur Yorinks	X		X	X	X	
26	Bernard Wiseman	X		X	X	X	
27	Graham Oakley	X	X		X	X	X
28	Roger Duvoisin	X	X	X	X	X	
28	Beau Gardner	X	X	X	X	X	
28	Tasha Tudor	X	X	X	X	X	

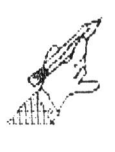

MARY CALHOUN

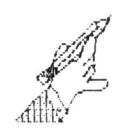

Jack and the Whoopie Wind

Read *Jack and the Whoopie Wind*. Match the words from the Word Bank to their meanings below.

1. __ __ __ __ __ __   wind
2. __ __ __ __   no hair
3. __ __ __   cools you off
4. __ __ __ __ __ __   put these on a mattress
5. __ __ __ __   fill up
6. __ __ __ __ __ __   rope
7. __ __ __ __ __ __   see movies on it
8. __ __ __ __ __ __   dig with this
9. __ __ __ __ __ __ __ __   makes the wind work
10. __ __ __ __ __ __   windy state

Word Bank

bald	breeze	fan	lariat	plug
screen	sheets	shovel	windmill	Wyoming

Name _____ Date _____

NANCY WHITE CARLSTROM

Better Not Get Wet, Jesse Bear

Read *Better Not Get Wet, Jesse Bear.* Use the words in the Word Bank to finish the sentences about a sweet little bear who has to wait to get wet in a special way.

1. Jesse drank _____ from a cup.
2. She tried to _____ the dishes.
3. Jesse tried to _____ the goldfish.
4. Dad was watering the _____.
5. Jesse _____ with the _____.
6. Jesse splashed a _____.
7. Dad filled the watering _____.
8. Jesse watered a _____.
9. Dad filled the _____ _____.
10. Now Jesse CAN get _____.

Word Bank

| bird | can | catch | danced | hose | juice |
| pool | roses | swimming | wash | wet | worm |

Name _____ Date _____

BARBARA COONEY
Island Boy

Read *Island Boy*. Barbara Cooney shows how an island is the home for many generations of Tibbets. Draw a family tree to show how long the Tibbets family lived on the island. This story covers many generations.

The story starts with a Matthias with eleven brothers and sisters. It ends with one Matthias, or does it? After you draw the family tree, write several sentences on the back of this sheet about the last Matthias. Will he stay on the island or not?

Name _____ Date _____

PATRICIA MCKISSACK

Mirandy and Brother Wind

Read *Mirandy and Brother Wind*. This story by Particia and pictures by Jerry Pinkney won a Caldecott Honor Medal. It is a wonderful, colorful tale of a traditional Southern pasttime of years gone by. Jerry's pictures are light as air and as beautiful as a sunny day.

Mirandy asked Brother Wind a favor. But Patricia did not share this dialog between Mirandy and Brother Wind. Write the dialog that could have happened. We know Mirandy wanted to win the cakewalk with Ezel, but he was so clumsy. How did they do it? Use the lines below for your rough draft ideas of the dialog. Pick a partner and present your dialog to the class.

_____

_____

_____

_____

_____

_____

_____

_____

Name _____ **Date** _____

JOSE ARUEGO / ARIANE DEWEY ARUEGO

How the Sun Was Brought Back to the Sky

Read *How the Sun Was Brought Back to the Sky* by Mirra Ginsburg. This story has two special illustrators. Not only were they born in the same month, they are married to one another. Do these pictures remind you of other pictures—Robert Kraus' books? Yes—they also drew pictures for Robert's books. Finish these sentences with words from the Word Bank.

1. The sun disappeared behind _____ for three days.

2. The chicks were _____.

3. They _____ to find the sun.

4. They asked a _____ but he said ask the magpie.

5. Magpie didn't know. He said ask the _____.

6. He didn't know. He said ask the _____.

7. He didn't know. He said ask the _____.

8. They rode a cloud to the _____.

9. It took them to the _____ of the sun.

10. The sun forgot how to _____.

11. Everyone _____ him and he shined again.

12. The chicks were _____ again.

Word Bank

cleaned	clouds	decided	duck	happy	hedgehog
house	moon	rabbit	sad	shine	snail

Name _____   Date _____

DON FREEMAN

Corduroy; A Pocket for Corduroy

Read *Corduroy* and *A Pocket for Corduroy*. Lisa and Corduroy are friends. In the first book, Lisa buys Corduroy. In the second, Lisa makes him a pocket. But what if . . .

Write a story about Lisa and Corduroy. What if Lisa's aunt comes to visit and brings Lisa a NEW teddy bear? What if she brings Lisa a NEW doll? What if . . . Write a story about Corduroy's reaction. Will Corduroy get along with the new toy in the house? What will the new toy think of him? Use the lines below to write down ideas for your rough draft.

_____

_____

_____

_____

_____

_____

_____

_____

_____

Name _____ **Date** _____

JOANNA COLE

Bony Legs

Read *Bony Legs*. Use the words in the Word Bank to finish these sentences about a little girl who defeats a nasty old witch.

1. Bony Legs was a _____.
2. Her teeth were made of _____.
3. She liked to eat _____.
4. Sasha went to borrow a _____ and _____.
5. She greased the noisy _____.
6. She gave _____ to the _____.
7. She gave _____ to the cat.
8. The cat gave Sasha a _____.
9. The dog gave Sasha a wooden _____.
10. The mirror turned into a _____.
11. The comb turned into very tall _____.
12. Sasha never saw _____ _____ again.

Word Bank				
bony	bread	children	comb	dog
gate	iron	lake	legs	meat
mirror	needle	thread	trees	witch

Name _____   Date _____

AUDREY WOOD

<u>Heckedy Peg</u>

    Read *Heckedy Peg*. Audrey's witch is not the only one who can change people into things. Try your hand at writing magic.
    Pick five of your friends. What could you turn them into? Give a reason for the thing they would become.

1. _____ would be a _____ because
_____

2. _____ would be a _____ because
_____

3. _____ would be a _____ because
_____

4. _____ would be a _____ because
_____

5. _____ would be a _____ because
_____

Name _____   **Date** _____

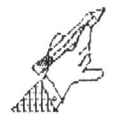

X. J. KENNEDY

Brats

Read *Brats*. These short little poems remind me of the poems in *Beastly Boys and Ghastly Girls* collected by William Cole.

Write a poem about a brat. This fictional kid does something wrong and gets it good. Write another poem about the same kid when he or she happens to be an angel. The good and the bad. We all make mistakes. Put all the *Brat* poems together in a book. Put all the *Angel* poems together in a book. Happy reading! Use the lines below to write down ideas for your rough draft.

Name _____ **Date** _____

BERNARD WISEMAN

Morris Tells Boris Mother Moose Stories and Rhymes

    Read *Morris Tells Boris Mother Moose Stories and Rhymes*. Morris and Boris were in these short silly stories. Let's make you a fairy tale character, too! Fill in these story blanks to make this story about you. This will help you get started. Put your finished story on another piece of paper.

    To make this story yours, you don't need to find a harp, bags of gold, and a giant above the clouds. When you climb the beanstalk, you can find whatever you want. Think about what you will find. Think about who or what might be up there. All the choices are yours. Have fun!

_____
and the Beanstalk

Once upon a time, there lived a little _____ named

_____. _____ was very poor. Only

the family _____ was left to sell. _____

took the _____ to town. _____

met a peddler. _____ traded the

_____ for magic beans. Mom was very angry.

_____ was sent to bed with no supper. Out the window

flew the beans. In the morning . . .

Name _____   Date _____

GRAHAM OAKLEY

The Church Mice at Bay

Read *The Church Mice at Bay*. Some of the words in this story are words from England. Match the words from the Word Bank to their meanings below.

1. __ __ __ __ __   minister

2. __ __ __ __ __ __ __ __   minister's house

3. __ __ __ __ __ __   vicar's helper

4. __ __ __ __   man or boy

5. __ __ __ __   form of concentration

6. __ __ __ __ __ __   special room in a church

7. __ __ __ __ __ __ __ __   wide-sleeved gown

8. __ __ __ __   church song

9. __ __ __ __ __ __   holy

10. __ __ __ __ __ __   rodents, mice

11. __ __ __ __ __ __ __   nasty name for a cat

12. __ __ __ __ __ __ __   vacation

Word Bank

| chap | curate | fleabag | holiday | hymn | sacred |
| surplice | vermin | vestry | vicar | vicarage | yoga |

Name _____ Date _____

BEAU GARDNER

The Look Again... and Again, and Again, and Again Book

Look at all the pictures in *The Look Again . . . and Again, and Again, and Again Book.* Each picture can be four things. Pick your favorite picture and make a copy of it for your wall at school or at home.

Make a picture with bright colors. See if you can call it four different things as you turn it. Use the space below for ideas for your own *Look Again* picture.

Name _____   Date _____

August Primary I

- Frank Asch
- Robert Bright
- Betsy Byars
- Laurent DeBrunhoff
- Don Freeman
- James Howe
- Audrey Wood
- Arthur Yorinks
- Nancy White Carlstrom
- Joanna Cole
- Jose & Ariane Aruego

August Primary II

- Mary Calhoun
- Joanna Cole
- Robert Crowe
- Roger Duvoisin
- Steven Kroll
- Trinka Hakes Noble
- Brinton Turkle
- Bernard Wiseman
- Barbara Cooney
- Patricia McKissack
- Jan Pienkowski

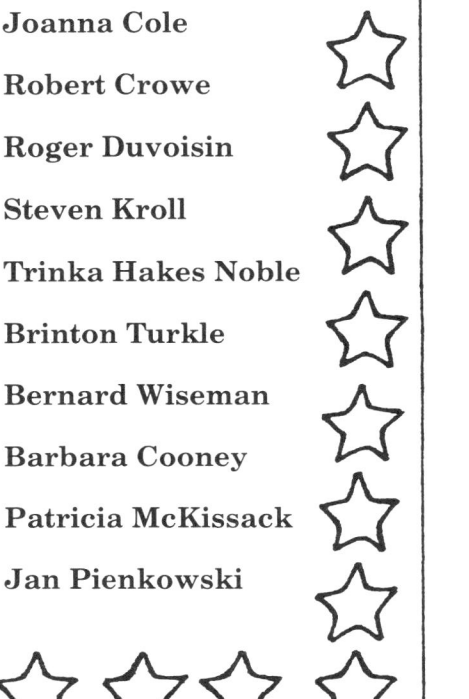

August Intermediate

- Betsy Byars
- Mary Calhoun
- Matt Christopher
- Deborah Howe
- James Howe
- Graham Oakley
- X. J. Kennedy
- Ruth Radlauer

AUGUST ANSWER KEY

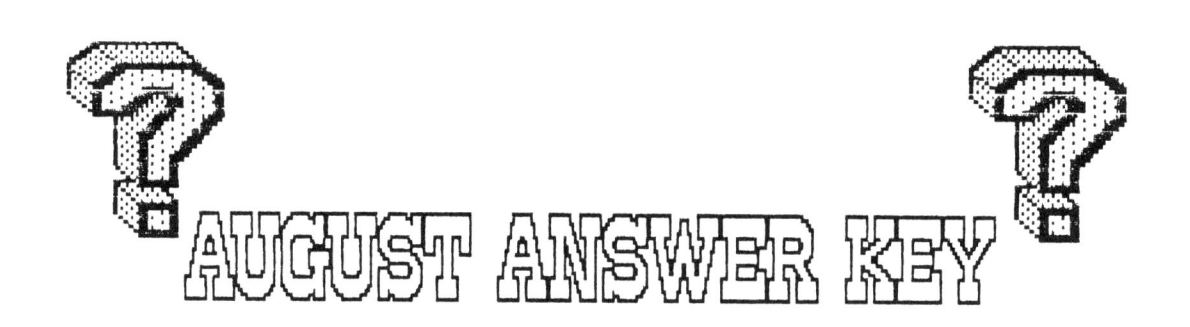

Mary Calhoun: *Jack and the Whoopie Wind*

1. breeze
2. bald
3. fan
4. sheets
5. plug
6. lariat
7. screen
8. shovel
9. windmill
10. Wyoming

Nancy White Carlstrom: *Better Not Get Wet, Jesse Bear*

1. juice
2. wash
3. catch
4. roses
5. danced, hose
6. bird
7. can
8. worm
9. swimming pool
10. wet

Jose Aruego/Ariane Dewey Aruego: *How the Sun Was Brought Back to the Sky*

1. clouds
2. sad
3. decided
4. snail
5. rabbit
6. duck
7. hedgehog
8. moon
9. house
10. shine
11. cleaned
12. happy

Joanna Cole: *Bony Legs*

1. witch
2. iron
3. children
4. needle, thread
5. gate
6. meat, dog
7. bread
8. mirror
9. comb
10. lake
11. trees
12. Bony Legs

August Answer Key

Graham Oakley: *The Church Mice at Bay*

1. vicar
2. vicarage
3. curate
4. chap
5. yoga
6. vestry
7. surplice
8. hymn
9. sacred
10. vermin
11. fleabag
12. holiday

AUGUST AUTHORS BIBLIOGRAPHY

August 3 Mary Calhoun
Another intermediate author adds her flair to the K-3 scene: *Wobble the Witch Cat* (Morrow, 1958); *Hungry Leprechaun* (Morrow, 1962); *The Witch of Hissing Hill* (Morrow, 1964); *Cross-Country Cat* (Morrow, 1979); *The Witch Who Lost Her Shadow* (Harper, 1979); *Audubon Cat* (Morrow, 1981); *Hot-Air Henry* (Morrow, 1981); *Jack and the Whoopie Wind* (Morrow, 1987)

August 4 Nancy White Carlstrom
All published by Macmillan: *Jesse Bear, What Will You Wear?* (1986); *The Moon Came Too* (1987); *Wild Wild Sunflower Child Anna* (1987); *Better Not Get Wet, Jesse Bear* (1988); *Graham Cracker Animals 1-2-3* (1989)

August 6 Barbara Cooney
The Little Juggler (Hastings, 1961); *Christmas* (Harper, 1967); *Miss Rumphius* (Penguin, 1982); *Island Boy* (Penguin, 1988)

August 9 Patricia McKissack
She writes for all levels with her husband Frederick and also as a single author: *Mirandy and Brother Wind* (Knopf, 1988)—1989 Caldecott Honor Book; beginning-to-read books published by Children's Press: *Who Is Who?* (1983); *Cinderella* (1985); *Country Mouse and City Mouse* (1985); *The Little Red Hen* (1985); *King Midas and His Gold* (1986); *The King's New Clothes* (1986); *Who Is Coming?* (1986); *Messy Bessey* (1987); *Three Billy Goats Gruff* (1987); *Bugs!* (1988); books about Native Americans for grades 2-3 published by Children's Press: *Apache* (1984); *Aztec* (1984); *Inca* (1985); *Maya* (1985); *Big Bug Book of . . .* series published by Milliken (1987): *Big Bug Book of the Alphabet; Big Bug Book of Opposites; Big Bug Book of Places to Go; Big Bug Book of Things to Do; Reading Well* series published by Milliken: *A Real Winner* (1987); *Tall Phil and Small Bill* (1987)

August 9 Jose Aruego with Ariane Dewey Aruego (August 17)
Crocodile's Tale (Scholastic, 1976); *Look What I Can Do* (Macmillan, 1988); *Rockabye Crocodile* (Greenwillow, 1988); *We Hide, You Seek* (Morrow, 1988); illustrated many of Robert Kraus's books: *Whose Mouse Are You?* (Macmillan, 1970); *Leo the Late Bloomer* (Crowell, 1971); *Herman the Helper* (Windmill, 1974); *Owliver* (Windmill, 1974); *Milton the Early Riser* (Messner, 1981); illustrated Mirra Ginsburg's books: *How the Sun Was Brought Back to the Sky* (Macmillan, 1975); *Where Does the Sun Go at Night* (Greenwillow, 1980)

August Authors Bibliography

August 11 Don Freeman

Fly High, Fly Low (Viking, 1957)—1958 Caldecott Honor Book; all published by Viking-Penguin: *Norman the Doorman* (1959); *Dandelion* (1964); *A Rainbow of My Own* (1966); *Corduroy* (1968); *Tilly Witch* (1969); *Will's Quill* (1970); *A Pocket for Corduroy* (1978); *Space Witch* (1979)

August 11 Joanna Cole

Magic Schoolbus series illustrated by Bruce Deegen and published by Scholastic: *Magic Schoolbus Inside the Earth* (1987); *Magic Schoolbus at the Water Works* (1988); *Magic Schoolbus Inside the Human Body* (1989); *Magic Schoolbus Lost in the Solar System* (1990); *Golly Gump Swallowed a Fly* (Parents, 1982); *Bony Legs* (Macmillan, 1983); *Monster Manners* (Scholastic, 1985); *Monster Movie* (Scholastic, 1987); the *Clown-Arounds* series published by Dutton: *The Clown-Arounds* (1981); *The Clown-Arounds Have a Party* (1982); *The Clown-Arounds Go on Vacation* (1984); *Get Well, Clown-Arounds!* (1987)

August 12 Audrey Wood

Tugford Wanted to Be Bad (HBJ, 1983); with Don Wood as illustrator and published by HBJ: *Napping House* (1984); *King Bidgood's in the Bathtub!* (1985); *Moonflute* (1986); *Heckedy Peg* (1987); *Elbert's Bad Word* (1988); with Don Wood as illustrator and published by Playspaces: *Quick as a Cricket* (1982); *The Big Hungry Bear* (1984); *Three Sisters* (Dial, 1986)

August 21 X. J. Kennedy

The Forgetful Wishing Well (Macmillan, 1985); *Knock at a Star: Child's Introduction to Poetry* (Little, Brown, 1985); *Brats* (Macmillan, 1986); *Ghastlies, Goops, and Pincushions: Nonsense Verse* (Macmillan, 1989)

August 26 Bernard Wiseman

Morris the Moose and Boris the Bear series: *Morris Goes to School* (Harper, 1970); *Morris and Boris* (Dodd, 1974); *Halloween with Morris and Boris* (Dodd, 1975); *Morris Tells Boris Mother Moose Stories and Rhymes* (Dodd, 1979)

August 27 Graham Oakley

The *Church Mice* series published by Macmillan: *The Church Mice at Bay* (1972); *The Church Mouse* (1972); *Church Cat* (1973); *The Church Mice and the Moon* (1974); *The Church Mice Adrift* (1977); *Church Cat Abroad* (1980); *The Church Mice at Christmas* (1980); *The Church Mice in Action* (1983); *Diary of a Church Mouse* (1987); a most ingenious book is *Magical Changes* (Macmillan, 1980) in which the pages are split to make different pictures.

August 28   Beau Gardner

The Turn About, Think About, Look About Book (Lothrop, 1980); *The Look Again, and Again, and Again, and Again Book* (Lothrop, 1984); *Guess What?* (Lothrop, 1985); *Have You Ever Seen? An ABC Book* (Putnam, 1986); *Can You Imagine?* (Putnam, 1987)

APPENDICES:

1. ALPHABETICAL AUTHORS
2. AUTHORS BY BIRTHDATES
3. TITLE INDEX
4. TOPICAL INDEX

ALPHABETICAL AUTHORS

A
Karen Ackerman, October 9
Phyllis Adams, December 5
Arnold Adoff, July 16
Allan Ahlberg, June 5
Janet Ahlberg, October 21
Aliki, September 3
Lonzo Anderson, March 1
Jose Aruego, August 9
Ariane Dewey Aruego, August 17

B
Natalie Babbitt, July 28
Edith Baer, April 29
Alan Baker, November 14
Molly Bang, December 29
Ron Barrett, July 25
Byron Barton, September 8
Byrd Baylor, March 28
Nathaniel Benchley, November 13
Barbara Berger, March 1
Franz Brandenberg, February 10
Jan Brett, December 1
Gwendolyn Brooks, June 7
Marcia Brown, July 13
Anthony Browne, September 11
Clyde Robert Bulla, January 9

C
Mary Calhoun, August 3
Stephanie Calmenson, November 28
Polly Cameron, October 14
Nancy White Carlstrom, August 4
Rebecca Caudill, February 2
Victoria Chess, November 16
Ruth Chew, April 8
Kay Chorao, January 7
Eileen Christelow, April 22
Mary Blount Christian, February 20
Lucille Clifton, June 27
Elizabeth Coatsworth, May 31
Brock Cole, May 29
Joanna Cole, August 11
William Cole, November 20
Peter Collington, April 2
David R. Collins, February 29
Barbara Cooney, August 6
Stephen Cosgrove, July 26
Bruce Coville, May 16

D
Bruce Degen, June 14
Lulu Delacre, October 20
Ida De Lage, July 16
Demi, September 2
Tomie de Paola, September 15

E
Lois Ehlert, November 9
Amy Ehrlich, July 24
Judith Elkin, June 7

F
Douglas Florian, March 18
Mem Fox, March 5
Don Freeman, August 11
Jean Fritz, November 16

G
Wanda Gag, March 11
Stephen Gammell, February 10
Ruth Stiles Gannett, December 16
Beau Gardner, August 28
Diane Goode, September 14
Nigel Gray, April 9
Eloise Greenfield, May 17
Barbara Gregorich, December 10
Fred Gwynne, July 10

H
Dorothy Haas, June 17
Kathleen Hague, March 6
Michael Hague, September 8
Gail Haley, November 4
Donald Hall, September 20

Phyllis Halloran, May 21
Bobbie Hamsa, June 14
Kevin Henkes, November 27
Margaret Hillert, January 22
John Himmelman, October 3
Adelaide Holl, December 9
Thacher Hurd, March 6
Pat Hutchins, June 18
Trina Schart Hyman, April 8

J

Susan Jeffers, October 7
Tony Johnston, January 30
Ann Jonas, January 28
Mavis Jukes, May 3

K

Ezra Jack Keats, March 11
Charles Keller, March 30
True Kelley, February 25
X. J. Kennedy, August 21
Fernando Krahn, January 4

L

Maria Leach, April 30
Hugh Lewin, December 3
Reeve Lindbergh, October 2
Henry Wadsworth Longfellow,
　　February 27

M

David Macaulay, December 2
Giulio Maestro, May 6
Jean Marzollo, June 24
Patricia McKissack, August 9
Lilian Moore, March 17
Elaine Moore, May 31
Stephen Mooser, July 4
Robert Munsch, June 11
Margaret Musgrove, November 19

N

Clare Turlay Newberry, April 10
Laura Joffe Numeroff, July 14

O

Graham Oakley, August 27
Edward Ormondroyd, October 8

P

Tony Palazzo, April 7
Peter Parnall, May 23
Jerry Pinkney, December 22
Charlotte Pomerantz, July 24

R

Ted Rand, December 27
Ellen Raskin, March 13
Nicole Rubel, April 29
Cynthia Rylant, June 6

S

Robert San Souci, October 10
Alvin Schwartz, April 25
John Scieszka, September 8
Ann H. Scott, November 19
Millicent Selsam, May 30
Maurice Sendak, June 10
Uri Shulevitz, February 27
David Small, February 12
John Steptoe, September 14
James Stevenson, July 11
Cyndy Szekeres, October 31

T

Ann Tompert, January 11

V

Judith Viorst, February 2

W

Jan Wahl, April 1
Lynd Ward, June 26
Ellen Weiss, December 7
Kurt Wiese, April 22
Brian Wildsmith, January 22
Hans Wilhelm, September 21
Barbara Williams, January 1
Vera B. Williams, January 28
Paula Winter, October 25
Bernard Wiseman, August 26
Audrey Wood, August 12

Y

Taro Yashima, September 21
Ed Young, November 28

AUTHORS BY BIRTHDATES

JANUARY
Barbara Williams, January 1
Fernando Krahn, January 4
Kay Chorao, January 7
Clyde Robert Bulla, January 9
Ann Tompert, January 11
Margaret Hillert, January 22
Brian Wildsmith, January 22
Ann Jonas, January 28
Vera B. Williams, January 28
Tony Johnston, January 30

FEBRUARY
Rebecca Caudill, February 2
Judith Viorst, February 2
Franz Brandenberg, February 10
Stephen Gammell, February 10
David Small, February 12
Mary Blount Christian, February 20
True Kelley, February 25
Henry Wadsworth Longfellow, February 27
Uri Shulevitz, February 27
David R. Collins, February 29

MARCH
Lonzo Anderson, March 1
Barbara Berger, March 1
Mem Fox, March 5
Kathleen Hague, March 6
Thacher Hurd, March 6
Wanda Gag, March 11
Ezra Jack Keats, March 11
Ellen Raskin, March 13
Lilian Moore, March 17
Douglas Florian, March 18
Byrd Baylor, March 28
Charles Keller, March 30

APRIL
Jan Wahl, April 1
Peter Collington, April 2
Tony Palazzo, April 7
Ruth Chew, April 8
Trina Schart Hyman, April 8
Nigel Gray, April 9
Clare Turlay Newberry, April 10
Eileen Christelow, April 22
Kurt Wiese, April 22
Alvin Schwartz, April 25
Edith Baer, April 29
Nicole Rubel, April 29
Maria Leach, April 30

MAY
Mavis Jukes, May 3
Giulio Maestro, May 6
Bruce Coville, May 16
Eloise Greenfield, May 17
Phyllis Halloran, May 21
Peter Parnall, May 23
Brock Cole, May 29
Millicent Selsam, May 30
Elizabeth Coatsworth, May 31
Elaine Moore, May 31

JUNE
Allan Ahlberg, June 5
Cynthia Rylant, June 6
Gwendolyn Brooks, June 7
Judith Elkin, June 7
Maurice Sendak, June 10
Robert Munsch, June 11
Bobbie Hamsa, June 14
Bruce Degen, June 14
Dorothy Haas, June 17
Pat Hutchins, June 18
Jean Marzollo, June 24
Lynd Ward, June 26
Lucille Clifton, June 27

JULY
Stephen Mooser, July 4
Fred Gwynne, July 10
James Stevenson, July 11
Marcia Brown, July 13

Laura Joffe Numeroff, July 14
Arnold Adoff, July 16
Ida De Lage, July 16
Amy Ehrlich, July 24
Charlotte Pomerantz, July 24
Ron Barrett, July 25
Stephen Cosgrove, July 26
Natalie Babbitt, July 28

AUGUST
Mary Calhoun, August 3
Nancy White Carlstrom, August 4
Barbara Cooney, August 6
Jose Aruego, August 9
Patricia McKissack, August 9
Joanna Cole, August 11
Don Freeman, August 11
Audrey Wood, August 12
Ariane Dewey Aruego, August 17
X. J. Kennedy, August 21
Bernard Wiseman, August 26
Graham Oakley, August 27
Beau Gardner, August 28

SEPTEMBER
Demi, September 2
Aliki, September 3
Byron Barton, September 8
Michael Hague, September 8
John Scieszka, September 8
Anthony Browne, September 11
Diane Goode, September 14
John Steptoe, September 14
Tomie de Paola, September 15
Donald Hall, September 20
Hans Wilhelm, September 21
Taro Yashima, September 21

OCTOBER
Reeve Lindbergh, October 2
John Himmelman, October 3
Susan Jeffers, October 7
Edward Ormondroyd, October 8
Karen Ackerman, October 9
Robert San Souci, October 10
Polly Cameron, October 14
Lulu Delacre, October 20

Janet Ahlberg, October 21
Paula Winter, October 25
Cyndy Szekeres, October 31

NOVEMBER
Gail Haley, November 4
Lois Ehlert, November 9
Nathaniel Benchley, November 13
Alan Baker, November 14
Victoria Chess, November 16
Jean Fritz, November 16
Margaret Musgrove, November 19
Ann H. Scott, November 19
William Cole, November 20
Kevin Henkes, November 27
Stephanie Calmenson, November 28
Ed Young, November 28

DECEMBER
Jan Brett, December 1
David Macaulay, December 2
Hugh Lewin, December 3
Phyllis Adams, December 5
Ellen Weiss, December 7
Adelaide Holl, December 9
Barbara Gregorich, December 10
Ruth Stiles Gannett, December 16
Jerry Pinkney, December 22
Ted Rand, December 27
Molly Bang, December 29

TITLE INDEX

A

Alexander & the Terrible, Horrible No Good Very Bad Day by Judith Viorst
Alphabears illustrated by Michael Hague
Amanda and the Witch Switch by John Himmelman
Angel and the Soldier Boy by Peter Collington
Animals Should Definitely Not Act Like People by Ron and Judi Barrett
April's Kittens by Clare T. Newberry
Arroz Con Leche by Lulu Delacre
Ashanti to Zulu by Margaret Musgrove

B

Bear and the Fly by Paula Winter
Bear Hugs by Kathleen Hague
Beauty and the Beast by Jan Brett
Benjamin's Portrait by Alan Baker
Best Present Ever by Jean Marzollo
Better Not Get Wet, Jesse Bear by Nancy White Carlstrom
The Biggest Bear by Lynd Ward
Black and White by David Macaulay
Bony Legs by Joanna Cole
The Boy Who Didn't Believe in Spring by Lucille Clifton
Brats by X. J. Kennedy
Broderick by Edward Ormondroyd
Bronzeville Boys and Girls by Gwendolyn Brooks
Bunnies All Day Long by Amy Ehrlich
Buzz, Buzz, Buzz by Byron Barton

C

Cat Purrs by Phyllis Halloran
The Cat Who Went to Heaven by Elizabeth Coatsworth
Certain Small Shepherd by Rebecca Caudill
Chalk Doll by Charlotte Pomerantz
Chicken Soup with Rice by Maurice Sendak
Chocolate Moose for Dinner by Fred Gwynne
Church Mice at Bay by Graham Oakley
Corduroy by Don Freeman
Country Crossing illustrated by Ted Rand
Country Far Away by Nigel Gray

D

Dandelion Hill by Robert Clyde Bulla
Dear Dragon series by Margaret Hillert
Devil's Storybook by Natalie Babbitt
Digging Up Dinosaurs by Aliki Brandenberg

E

Eating the Alphabet by Lois Ehlert
Emma by James Stevenson

F

Family in Japan by Judith Elkin
Farmer and the Witch by Ida DeLage
Ferryboat by Giulio Maestro
Fish in the Air by Kurt Wiese
Five Little Monkeys Jumping on the Bed by Eileen Christelow
Funnybones by Allan Ahlberg

G

George Told Kate by Kay Chorao
Giant's Toe by Brock Cole
Goggles by Ezra Jack Keats
Grandfather Tang's Story by Ann Tompert
Grandfather Twilight by Barbara Berger

Grandfather Woo Goes to School by David R. Collins
Great Fish by Peter Parnall
Guess What? by Mem Fox
Gwinna by Barbara Berger

H

Happy Birthday, Mole and Troll by Tony Johnston
Heckedy Peg by Audrey and Don Wood
Hi, Dog! by Phyllis Adams
Hiawatha by Henry Wadsworth Longfellow, illustrated by Susan Jeffers
Honey, I Love by Eloise Greenfield
How the Sun Was Brought Back to the Sky illustrated by Jose Aruego and Ariane Dewey Aruego
Humphrey's Bear by Jan Wahl

I

I Can't Said the Ant by Polly Cameron
I Hear a Noise by Diane Goode
I'll Always Love You by Hans Wilhelm
I'm in Charge of Celebrations by Byrd Baylor
If You Give a Mouse a Cookie by Laura Joffe Numeroff
Imogene's Antlers by David Small
In a Dark, Dark Room and Other Scary Stories by Alvin Schwartz
In for Winter, Out for Spring by Arnold Adoff
Island Boy by Barbara Cooney

J

Jack and the Whoopie Wind by Mary Calhoun
Jafta's Father by Hugh Lewin
"Jemima" by Henry Wadsworth Longfellow
The Jolly Postman or Other People's Letters by Janet Ahlberg

K

Kevin's Grandma by Barbara Williams
The King Who Rained by Fred Gwynne

L

Lazy Bear by Brian Wildsmith
Legend of Scarface by Robert San Souci
Legend of the Indian Paintbrush by Tomie DePaola
Leo and Emily's Big Ideas by Franz Brandenberg
Liang and the Magic Paintbrush by Demi
Like Jake and Me by Mavis Jukes
A Little Pigeon Toad by Fred Gwynne
Little Red Riding Hood illustrated by Trina Schart Hyman
Lon Po Po by Ed Young
The Look Again, and Again, and Again, and Again Book by Beau Gardner
Love You Forever by Robert Munsch

M

Magic Schoolbus Inside the Human Body by Joanna Cole, illustrated by Bruce Degen
The Magician by Uri Shulevitz
Mama Don't Allow by Thacher Hurd
Mice at Bat by True Kelley
Midnight Farm by Reeve Lindbergh, illustrated by Susan Jeffers
Millicent Maybe by Ellen Weiss
Millions of Cats by Wanda Gag
Mirandy and Brother Wind by Patricia McKissack
Mixed-Up Sam by Elaine Moore
More, More, More Said the Baby by Vera B. Williams
Morris Tells Boris Mother Moose Stories and Rhymes by Bernard Wiseman
Moving Day by Cyndy Szekeres

Title Index

Mufaro's Beautiful Daughters by John Steptoe
My Father's Dragon by Ruth Stiles Gannett
My Halloween Boyfriend by Stephen Mooser
Mystery of the Giant Footprints by Fernando Krahn

N

New Friends by Dorothy Haas
Night in the Country by Cynthia Rylant
Nine Men Chase a Hen by Barbara Gregorich
No Such Thing as a Witch by Ruth Chew
Nothing Ever Happens on My Block by Ellen Raskin

O

On Christmas Eve by Peter Collington
Once Around the Block by Kevin Henkes
Ox-Cart Man by Donald Hall

P

Pet Day Mystery by Mary Blount Christian
Pocket for Corduroy by Don Freeman
Poem Stew by William Cole
Pretend You're a Cat illustrated by Jerry Pinkney
The Principal's New Clothes by Stephanie Calmenson

R

Rain Puddle by Adelaide Holl
Reflections by Ann Jonas
Relatives Came illustrated by Stephen Gammell
Round Trip by Ann Jonas

S

Sam by Ann H. Scott
Sarah and the Dragon by Bruce Coville
Sarah's Unicorn by Bruce Coville
See My Lovely Poison Ivy by Lilian Moore
Shadow illustrated by Marcia Brown
Shimmeree by Stephen Cosgrove
Song and Dance Man by Karen Ackerman illustrated by Stephen Gammell
A Story, A Story by Gail Haley
The Strange Disappearance of Arthur Cluck by Nathaniel Benchley

T

Talking Eggs by Robert San Souci
Ten, Nine, Eight by Molly Bang
The Tenth Good Thing About Barney by Judith Viorst
Terry and the Caterpillars by Millicent Selsam
The Thing at the Foot of the Bed by Maria Leach
This Is the Way We Go to School by Edith Baer
Timothy Turtle by Tony Palazzo
Tongue Twisters by Charles Keller
Trek by Ann Jonas
The True Story of the 3 Little Pigs by John Scieszka
Turtle Day by Douglas Florian
Two Hundred Rabbits by Lonzo Anderson

U

Umbrella by Taro Yashima
Uncle Henry and Aunt Henrietta's Honeymoon by Nicole Rubel

W

When the Sun Rose by Barbara Berger

Who's That Stepping on Plymouth Rock? by Jean Fritz

Willy the Wimp by Anthony Browne

The Wind Blew by Pat Hutchins

Y

Your Pet Elephant by Bobbie Hamsa

TOPICAL INDEX

AFRICA
Ashanti to Zulu by Margaret Musgrove 42*
A Country Far Away by Nigel Gray 136
Jafta's Father by Hugh Lewin 57

ALLIGATORS
Uncle Henry and Aunt Henrietta's Honeymoon by Nicole Rubel .. 143

THE ALPHABET
Alphabears illustrated by Michael Hague 7
Eating the Alphabet by Lois Ehlert 38

ANATOMY
Magic Schoolbus Inside the Human Body by Joanna Cole, illustrated by Bruce Degen .. 217

ANIMALS
Animals Should Definitely Not Act Like People by Ron and Judi Barrett 201

BEARS
Better Not Get Wet, Jesse Bear by Nancy White Carlstrom 212
The Biggest Bear by Lynd Ward .. 183
Corduroy by Don Freeman 216
The Lazy Bear by Brian Wildsmith 79
Morris Tells Boris Mother Moose Stories and Rhymes by Bernard Wiseman 220
Pocket for Corduroy by Don Freeman 216

BEDTIME
Humphrey's Bear by Jan Wahl ... 131
Midnight Farm by Reeve Lindbergh, illustrated by Susan Jeffers 21
Night in the Country by Cynthia Rylant 170
Ten, Nine, Eight by Molly Bang ... 66

BIRTHDAYS
Happy Birthday, Mole and Troll by Tony Johnston 82

CATS
April's Kittens by Clare T. Newberry 138
Millions of Cats by Wanda Gag .. 117

CHINA
Fish in the Air by Kurt Wiese ... 139
Liang and the Magic Paintbrush by Demi 3
Lon Po Po by Ed Young 46

CHRISTMAS
Best Present Ever by Jean Marzollo 181
Certain Small Shepherd by Rebecca Caudill 91

THE CITY
Goggles by Ezra Jack Keats 118

THE COUNTRY
Country Crossing illustrated by Ted Rand 65

COWS
Dandelion Hill by Clyde Robert Bulla 76

---

*Title/Author ... page number.

DEATH
I'll Always Love You by Hans Wilhelm 13
The Tenth Good Thing About Barney by Judith Viorst 93

DEVIL
Devil's Storybook by Natalie Babbit 203

DINOSAURS
Digging Up Dinosaurs by Aliki 4

DOLLS
Chalk Doll by Charlotte Pomerantz 200

DRAGONS
My Father's Dragon by Ruth Stiles Gannett 62
Sarah and the Dragon by Bruce Covill 153

EASY READERS
Dear Dragon series by Margaret Hillert 78
Hi, Dog! by Phyllis Adams 58
Leo and Emily's Big Ideas by Franz Brandenberg 94
Millicent Maybe by Ellen Weiss ... 59
Mixed-Up Sam by Elaine Moore 159
Nine Men Chase a Hen by Barbara Gregorich 61

ELEPHANTS
Your Pet Elephant by Bobbie Hamsa 175

THE ENGLISH LANGUAGE
Chocolate Moose for Dinner by Fred Gwynne 193
The King Who Rained by Fred Gwynne 193
A Little Pigeon Toad by Fred Gwynne 193
Tongue Twisters by Charles Keller 123

FAIRY TALES
Beauty and the Beast by Jan Brett 55
Bony Legs by Joanna Cole 217
The Cat Who Went to Heaven by Elizabeth Coatsworth 160
Giant's Toe by Brock Cole 157
Gwinna by Barbara Berger 112
The Jolly Postman or Other People's Letters by Janet Ahlberg 29
Little Red Riding Hood illustrated by Trina Schart Hyman 137
Lon Po Po by Ed Young 46
Mufaro's Beautiful Daughters by John Steptoe 10
The Principal's New Clothes by Stephanie Calmenson 47
Shimmeree by Stephen Cosgrove 202
A Story, A Story by Gail Haley ... 37
The True Story of the 3 Little Pigs by John Scieszka 6

FAMILY
Alexander & the Terrible, Horrible No Good Very Bad Day by Judith Viorst 92
George Told Kate by Kay Chorao .. 75
Like Jake and Me by Mavis Jukes 151
Love You Forever by Robert Munsch 174
More, More, More Said the Baby by Vera B. Williams 81
Sam by Ann H. Scott 43

FANTASY
Grandfather Twilight by Barbara Berger 111
Imogene's Antlers by David Small 96
Nothing Ever Happens on My Block by Ellen Raskin 119
Pretend You're a Cat illustrated by Jerry Pinkney 64
When the Sun Rose by Barbara Berger 111

Topical Index

FARMS
Buzz, Buzz, Buzz by Byron Barton . . 5
Rain Puddle by Adelaide Holl 60

FEELINGS
Umbrella by Taro Yashima 14

FRIENDSHIP
New Friends by Dorothy Haas . . . 177

GRANDFATHERS
Grandfather Tang's Story by Ann Tompert 77
Grandfather Woo Goes to School by David R. Collins 102
Song and Dance Man by Karen Ackerman 24

GRANDMOTHERS
Kevin's Grandma by Barbara Williams 73

HALLOWEEN
Funnybones by Allan Ahlberg . . . 169
My Halloween Boyfriend by Stephen Mooser 191

HAMSTERS
Benjamin's Portrait by Alan Baker 40

HISTORICAL
Ox-Cart Man by Donald Hall 12
Who's That Stepping on Plymouth Rock? by Jean Fritz 41

INSECTS
Terry and the Caterpillars by Millicent Selsam 158

ISLANDS
Island Boy by Barbara Cooney . . . 213

JAPAN
Family in Japan by Judith Elkin 172

LEGENDS
Great Fish by Peter Parnall 156
"Hiawatha" by Henry Wadsworth Longfellow, illustrated by Susan Jeffers 99
How the Sun Was Brought Back to the Sky illustrated by Jose Aruego and Ariane Dewey Aruego 215
Jack and the Whoopie Wind by Mary Calhoun 211
Legend of Scarface by Robert San Souci 25
Legend of the Indian Paintbrush by Tomie De Paola 11
Liang and the Magic Paintbrush by Demi 3
Magician by Uri Shulevitz 101
Mirandy and Brother Wind by Patricia McKissack 214
Shadow by Marcia Brown 195
Talking Eggs by Robert San Souci 26

MICE
Broderick by Edward Ormondroyd 23
Church Mice at Bay by Graham Oakley 221
If You Give a Mouse a Cookie by Laura Joffe Numeroff 196
Mice at Bat by True Kelley 98
Moving Day by Cyndy Szekeres . . . 31

MONKEYS
Willy The Wimp by Anthony Browne 8

MONSTERS
I Hear a Noise by Diane Goode 9
In a Dark, Dark Room and Other Scary Stories by Alvin Schwartz 141
The Thing at the Foot of the Bed by Maria Leach 144

MYSTERY
Pet Day Mystery by Mary Blount Christian 97

The Strange Disappearance of Arthur Cluck by Nathaniel Benchley 39

NATIVE AMERICANS
I'm in Charge of Celebrations by Byrd Baylor 122

POETRY
Bear Hugs by Kathleen Hague .. 116
Brats by X.J. Kennedy 219
Bronzeville Boys and Girls by Gwendolyn Brooks 171
Cat Purrs by Phyllis Halloran ... 155
Honey, I Love by Eloise Greenfield 154
In for Winter, Out for Spring by Arnold Adoff 197
"Jemima" by Henry Wadsworth Longfellow................ 100
Poem Stew by William Cole 44
See My Lovely Poison Ivy by Lilian Moore 120

PREDICTABLE BOOKS
Once Around the Block by Kevin Henkes.................... 45

RABBITS
Bunnies All Day Long by Amy Ehrlich................... 199
Two Hundred Rabbits by Lonzo Anderson 113

RHYMES
Chicken Soup with Rice by Maurice Sendak................... 173
Five Little Monkeys Jumping on the Bed by Eileen Christelow 140
I Can't Said the Ant by Polly Cameron 27

SONGS
Mama Don't Allow by Thacher Hurd..................... 115

SPAIN
Arroz Con Leche by Lulu Delacre 28

SPRING
The Boy Who Didn't Believe in Spring by Lucille Clifton 184

TRANSPORTATION
Ferryboat by Giulio Maestro..... 152
This Is the Way We Go to School by Edith Baer 142

TURTLES
Timothy Turtle by Tony Palazzo.. 133
Turtle Day by Douglas Florian .. 121

UNICORNS
Sarah's Unicorn by Bruce Coville 153

VACATIONS
Relatives Came illustrated by Stephen Gammell 95

VISUAL DELIGHTS
Black and White by David Macaulay 56
The Look Again, and Again, and Again, and Again Book by Beau Gardner 222
Reflections by Ann Jonas 80
Round Trip by Ann Jonas 80
Trek by Ann Jonas 80

WEATHER
The Wind Blew by Pat Hutchins 180

WITCHES
Amanda and the Witch Switch by John Himmelman........... 22
Bony Legs by Joanna Cole 217
Emma by James Stevenson 194
Farmer and the Witch by Ida DeLage................... 198
Guess What? by Mem Fox....... 114
Heckedy Peg by Audrey and Don Wood..................... 218

Topical Index

No Such Thing as a Witch by
    Ruth Chew............ 134, 135
See My Lovely Poison Ivy by Lilian
    Moore.................... 120

WORDLESS BOOKS

Angel and the Soldier Boy by Peter
    Collington 132

Bear and the Fly by Paula Winter 30
Mystery of the Giant Footprints by
    Fernando Krahn............ 74
On Christmas Eve by Peter
    Collington 132